1975

Mixed Doubles

Mixed Doubles

AN ENTERTAINMENT ON MARRIAGE BY

Alan Ayckbourn
John Bowen
Lyndon Brook
David Campton
George Melly
Alun Owen
Harold Pinter
James Saunders
Fay Weldon

METHUEN & CO LTD
11 NEW FETTER LANE · LONDON EC4

First published in 1970 by Methuen and Co Ltd.
Printed in Great Britain by
Cox & Wyman Ltd, Fakenham, Norfolk
SBN 416 16160 X

★

Applications for the right to perform individual plays from the *Mixed Doubles* sequence should be made as follows:
A Man's Best Friend and *Countdown*: to Margaret Ramsay Ltd.
Score: to Lynoq Productions Ltd., 87 Finlay Street, London S.W.6.
Norma: to Felix de Wolfe and Associates, 61 Berkeley House, 15 Hay Hill, London W.1.
Night and *Resting Place*: to Actac Ltd., 16 Cadogan Lane, London S.W.1.
Permanence: to Clive Goodwin Associates, 79 Cromwell Road, London S.W.7.
The linking sketches by George Melly: to P.L. Representation Ltd., 33 Sloane Street, London S.W.1.
The version of *Silver Wedding* by John Bowen included in *Mixed Doubles* and printed here is approximately half of a one-act play, of the same title, in two scenes, with two characters. Applications for performance, etc, of the full text should be made to Margaret Ramsay Ltd.

CONTENTS

Mixed Doubles was originally presented at the Hampstead Theatre Club on February 6 1969, under the title *We Who Are About To . . .* , and was subsequently presented in this final version at the Comedy Theatre, London on April 9 1969. The linking scenes written by George Melly were performed by Victor Maddern. The casts for the plays were as follows:

A MAN'S BEST FRIEND by James Saunders

JACKIE	Andree Melly
PETE	Oscar Quitak

SCORE by Lyndon Brook

HARRY	Nigel Stock
SHEILA	Vivien Merchant

NORMA by Alun Owen

THE WOMAN	Andree Melly
THE MAN	Oscar Quitak

NIGHT by Harold Pinter

THE WOMAN	Vivien Merchant
THE MAN	Nigel Stock

PERMANENCE by Fay Weldon

HELEN	Andree Melly
PETER	Oscar Quitak

COUNTDOWN by Alan Ayckbourn

THE HUSBAND	Nigel Stock
THE WIFE	Vivien Merchant

SILVER WEDDING by John Bowen

AUDREY	Andree Melly
JULIAN	Oscar Quitak

RESTING PLACE by David Campton

THE OLD WOMAN	Vivien Merchant
THE OLD MAN	Nigel Stock

Mixed Doubles was devised by Anton Rodgers and directed by Alexander Dore.
Designed by Tim Goodchild.
Lighting by Joe Davis.

Part One

THE VICAR

Speaking from the pulpit

. . . It seems but yesterday she was standing in front of this very altar holding the Brownie's banner at a service of dedication; and yet we are gathered here this day to witness her entry into the state of holy matrimony with the man of her choice.

I must confess that I hadn't met her husband-to-be before they came to discuss the arrangements yet, even on so short an acquaintance, I was impressed. A serious young man, practical yes, but very very much in love.

Today is a joyous day, and rightly so, yet I would be at fault if I were not to remind this young couple that the night cometh. Marriage is not all a bed of roses. There is no rose without a thorn. We are raised up through suffering, yet our faith penetrates the darkness like a great lighthouse. It is the upright mast to which we must nail our hopes. It bendeth, yet doth not break, though the faithless cry out or moan as the storm reaches a climax and the timbers creak beneath us.

Marriage is like unto a vineyard. Yea a vineyard where the good husbandman tendeth the vines with gloves on. We hear much of 'modern methods': the chemical sprays of permissiveness, the artificial manure of purely sensual pleasure. But Christ watches over the marriage bed. Not literally of course, but in spirit. This young couple before us are setting out on a pilgrimage and we must pray they don't fall by the wayside too often. Ideal love is pure, totally pure. In sickness and in health you will promise, and that means unselfishness, for the moon waneth and waxeth. Plenty of fresh vegetables and cold baths, not too many blankets is sound advice, as suitable at a wedding as for a confirmation class; and now let us sing hymn three hundred and twenty-seven: 'The Bridegroom cometh 'ere his time . . .'

A MAN'S BEST FRIEND

by *James Saunders*

Two benches set representing seats in a railway carriage.

BRIDE. We seem to have exhausted the conversation . . .

    Pause.

GROOM. What? . . .

BRIDE. Do you want a chocolate?

GROOM. No thank you, darling . . . (*He smiles, wanly.*)

BRIDE. It'll keep your strength up.

    His smile goes.

  As my Uncle George did nothing but say.

GROOM. Uncle George is a bit of a card.

BRIDE. Isn't he?

    Pause. He taps his foot on the floor.

GROOM. One doesn't take him seriously of course.

BRIDE. Don't tap your foot, darling.

GROOM. I'm not tapping my foot.

BRIDE. Darling, you are.

    He looks, stops tapping.

GROOM. Does it annoy you?

BRIDE. Of course not . . .

GROOM. This is the sort of thing one should be on the lookout for, you see. I'm glad you mentioned it. You must mention all those little things you find irritating or annoying. Because it's a well-known fact that it's those little things that wear a marriage down – (*He is tapping again.*)

BRIDE. It doesn't annoy me, darling. I'd just rather you didn't do it.

GROOM. Why?

BRIDE. It means you're worried.

GROOM. I tap my foot when I'm worried?

BRIDE. It was one of the first things I noticed about you. The first time . . . You took me to a restaurant you took one look at the wine list and away went your foot.

GROOM. You've never mentioned it before.

BRIDE. It's not important, darling, really. After all, it's part of you.

GROOM. My foot . . .

BRIDE. The way you tap it; it's part of your character. Like the way you walk.

Slight pause.

I mean it's *characteristic*. It makes you *belong* to me, you see? I could tell you in a thousand just by the way you walk.

Slight pause.

GROOM. Don't I walk normally?

BRIDE. It depends what you mean by normally, darling.

GROOM. What do *you* mean by normally?

BRIDE. There's some confetti on your lapel.

GROOM. Where?

BRIDE. It's not going to bite you. (*She flicks it off.*) There, it's off.

GROOM. I thought I'd got rid of all that stuff. Where's it gone?

BRIDE. What?

GROOM. That bit of confetti.

BRIDE. What do you want it for?

GROOM. I don't want it, I want to get rid of it.

BRIDE. But I've *got* rid of it.

GROOM. No you haven't you've flicked it onto the floor some- where. Or on the seat even. (*He gets up, starts searching.*) If someone comes in the compartment and sees that bit of confetti . . .

BRIDE. They'll know we're just married.

GROOM. Exactly.

BRIDE. So what?

He searches on hands and knees.

I *like* being married, I don't care who knows it.

GROOM. There's no need to shout it from the housetops, that we're just married . . .

BRIDE. Darling, we're talking about a little piece of confetti . . . it's on the seat.

GROOM. Where?

BRIDE. Just there, under your nose. I'll brush it off.

GROOM. No! (*He wets his finger, picks up the piece of confetti cautiously, opens the window and carefully lets it go. He sits down again.*) There.

BRIDE. How long do you mean to keep it a secret?

GROOM. I just don't want to brandish it about, darling, that's all. Surely you can understand that. It'll be bad enough having the whole of the hotel staff knowing we're newlyweds. They have second sight, those people.

BRIDE. We can tell them we're living in sin if you prefer. If it worries you.

GROOM. Worries me? It doesn't worry me. Why should it worry me?

BRIDE. That's what I wondered.

GROOM. It doesn't worry me, darling. I'm not a callow youth after all. Why should a thing like that worry me? It doesn't worry me . . . he ha . . .

BRIDE. You've made your point, darling.

GROOM. All I ask is that they give us service. That's what they're paid for. Let them do their job and let me do . . .

Pause.

BRIDE. Relax, darling. We're not going to the dentist's. Now you're biting your lip. Now you're tapping your foot again . . .

He uncrosses his other leg and puts his foot to the floor with a bang. There is a short moment of suspense. Then he reaches under his seat and brings out his guitar.

Do you want a magazine?

GROOM. No thank you very much. (*He opens the guitar case, rubs at a smudge with his sleeve, then takes out his breast-pocket handkerchief to polish it.*)

There is a shower of confetti.

Pause.

Very well. Let everybody know we're just married! (*He polishes his guitar; pauses.*) Does it annoy you that I bite my lip?

BRIDE. Darling, why should it annoy me? I simply don't like you *worrying* —

GROOM. I'm not worrying; I've nothing to worry *about*.

BRIDE. I know, I just thought you had.

Slight pause.

GROOM. What?

BRIDE. I don't know, darling. Do you?

He brushes confetti off his jacket and fiddles with the guitar.

BRIDE. Are you going to practise that thing now?

GROOM. I thought I'd just tune it up.

BRIDE. But you tuned it up half an hour ago.

GROOM. They get out of tune. (*He plucks a string.*)

BRIDE. Does it matter?

GROOM. Of course it matters.

BRIDE. You can't play it.

GROOM. I can't *learn* to play it if it's not tuned, can I? (*He plucks a string.*) The strings slacken. It happens on all guitars. You have to keep them tuned up. Every stringed instrument's the same. The strings slacken. I can't learn to play on slack strings. (*He plucks a string.*)

BRIDE. You're just tuning it up then putting it away?

He plucks a string.

So in half an hour'a time you'll take it out and tune it again?

Pause

Are you going to tune that guitar at half-hourly intervals throughout our honeymoon?

GROOM. If tuning this guitar *irritates* you . . .

BRIDE. I only want to know where I stand. If there's to be a third party . . . It also occurred to me that if someone looks in this compartment and sees you covered with confetti, tuning a guitar, it might look a little odd.

GROOM. What's odd about it? (*He plucks a string.*)

BRIDE. It's still flat. Now it's sharp . . . In fact the very idea of taking a guitar on a honeymoon seems a wee bit grotesque . . . when you can't play it. (*She giggles.*)

GROOM. I don't see anything grotesque about it. It seems perfectly natural to me.

BRIDE. Of course, a harp would be funnier still. I mean, serenading your lady outside her window would be very romantic, if you could play it, but tuning it up isn't quite the same . . .

GROOM. I happen to be very fond of my guitar.

BRIDE. Oh, darling . . .

GROOM. I mean I've got used to having it around. But if you object to it . . .

   She giggles.

BRIDE. Darling . . . You don't take it to bed with you?

   He gives a final twist to the screw.

   The string's snapped.

GROOM. I realize that. (*He puts the guitar away, deliberately.*)

BRIDE. You haven't finished tuning it.

GROOM. It doesn't matter.

BRIDE. Actually I'm crazy about guitar music. When it's well-played . . .

GROOM. I know. That's why I bought it in the first place.

   Pause.

BRIDE. Darling . . .

GROOM. But it doesn't matter. We all get delusions about ourselves. I pictured myself learning to play it really well, so I could . . . play it. It's a great asset, to be able to play an instrument. But since it obviously irritates you, I know better than to keep on with it. It's little irritations like that that wear a marriage down, and marriage comes first. I'll not let my guitar come between us. I'll not look at it again, I'll sell it.

BRIDE. Dar-ling . . .

GROOM. In any case, I'd never be any good at it. I mean not first rate. I'd never be better than second rate and I don't want to be second rate. I'm second rate at too many things already to be second rate at that as well. There's no point in going out of one's way to pile up things one's second rate at.

BRIDE. Darling, have I hurt . . . ?

GROOM. Hurt my feelings, what a crazy idea. D'you think I'm a child? I'm just facing facts, that's all. Facts are not always easy to face, not when you've set your heart on something, but it's best to face them in time. Before it's too late. (*He looks at his watch.*)

BRIDE. Another twenty-five minutes.

GROOM. What?

BRIDE. We'll be at the hotel in an hour.

GROOM. Then there's this business of morning tea. Why can't they leave the morning tea outside the door? I object to having strange women marching into my room first thing in the morning.

BRIDE. We don't *have* to have morning tea, darling.

GROOM. Ha ha, and have them wondering why we're *not* having morning tea.

BRIDE. Do you want a chocolate?

GROOM. As for that Uncle George of yours, he's on the way to becoming a dirty old man, that's my opinion.

BRIDE. He's travelled a lot in his time.

GROOM. That's no excuse. Apart from exaggerating . . .

BRIDE. What about?

GROOM. What about? He only talked about one thing. I've never heard anything like it.

BRIDE. I know he's a bit coarse, darling . . .

GROOM. Coarseness is one thing, I don't object to that; I've as many coarse relations as the next man; but making up wildly improbable stories about his . . . prowess, at his niece's wedding, that's something else.

BRIDE. Hmm.

    Pause.

GROOM. You mean you *believed* all those stories?

BRIDE. He's been married three times, darling.

GROOM. What's that got to do with it! Of course he was ex-aggerating . . . (*His foot taps. He recrosses his legs. The other foot taps.*)

BRIDE. You know best . . .

GROOM. What do you mean by that?

BRIDE. I don't mean anything, darling . . . Are you sure you don't want a chocolate?

GROOM. Why do you keep offering me chocolates? What are you insinuating?

BRIDE. Darling, I don't know what you mean. I didn't want to pig the whole box, that's all. You know what I'm like with chocolates . . . (*Pause. She leans back, closes her eyes.*) Did you know, darling . . . that when the cocoa-bean first found its way to this country . . . it was considered an aphrodisiac . . . ?

There is an awkward pause.

I don't know why that came into my mind . . .

Slight pause. He looks at his watch.

GROOM. Twenty three minutes . . .

BRIDE (*eyes closed*). What's it going to be like tomorrow, I wonder . . . (*Pause.*) Will it be like today, do you think? Or will it rain?

GROOM. How do I know, darling?

BRIDE (*eyes closed*). It's a funny time, isn't it, this journey-time . . . between the wedding reception and the . . . honeymoon hotel. Between one life and another. A bit sort of disjointed. Like a sort of limbo . . . I didn't expect it to be like this . . . ?

GROOM. I'll tell you the reason I'll never be a first class guitarist. It's because of my hands. There's nothing wrong with them as *hands* . . . They're just not the *sort* of hands that make anything but a second rate player. It's not my fault of course. I just have to realise my limitations . . . And not give any . . . false impressions . . . in advance . . .

Pause. They both jolt suddenly.

She opens her eyes.

Points.

BRIDE. Points?

GROOM. Points. We're on the outskirts . . .

BRIDE. I dropped off.

GROOM. Oh . . .

> *Slight pause. She puts out her hand.*
> *He stretches out his; she takes it.*
> *She examines the palm of his hands closely.*

BRIDE. You've got . . . nice hands . . .

GROOM. Darling . . .

BRIDE. Hm . . . ?

GROOM. What did you mean about the way I walk . . . ?

> *They freeze in profile as the sound of the train comes up.*
> *The lights fade to blackout.*

THE BANK MANAGER

The BANK MANAGER *is sitting behind his desk leafing through a statement. He looks up at an imaginary man seated in front of him.*
If it was up to me of course I wouldn't worry, but as you know our Lords and Masters aren't very keen on overdrafts at the moment and if all my customers have what they asked for they'd be down at me from head office like a ton of the proverbial bricks ha ha. Besides we do like to come to an arrangement and I don't believe we ever have. Just crept up on us hasn't it?
A pause.
Yes, I agree we took on the bridge loan but then, when you put your old house on the market you led us to believe that it'd cover the cost of the new one . . .
A pause.
Of course it wasn't your fault they decided to build an overpass right in front of your old house but then it wasn't ours was it?
Offers cigarette.
Cigarette? No? You'll stick to cigars.
Puts away case.
Yes I realise you had to move into a more select area now you've gone up in the world. I appreciate that, but two thousand on that bridge-loan-cum-overdraft in the last nine months . . .
A pause.
Oh no, there's no mistake. It's all down here in black and white . . . well red and white actually . . .
He glances down.
A new car I see; that's put the monthly payments up.
Short pause.
Yes, I do see that in your position you can't make do with an old car, but it's not only the car . . . There's a new standing order

at twenty pounds a week in favour of 'Fine Furs'. Eighteen months to go . . .

A short pause. He raises a placatory hand.

Hold on. I never suggested that your good lady should 'make do with a nylon fun fur' as you put it, but in your present financial position . . .

He glances down again.

. . . and thirty guineas per annum for the Greenways Golf Club. It's a very nice club they tell me, a very select club, but it does happen to be the most expensive club this side of Guildford.

A pause.

It may very well be necessary to join the right clubs. I can understand that. Yes . . .

Another glance.

Is the Pandora Club, Dean Street . . . Oh! Incidentally while we're on the subject are you intending to change your signature? Several of the cheques you've made out from there show considerable variation.

A pause.

Of course you're entitled to your relaxation. You've a great deal more responsibility and very clearly you would have an excellent future ahead of you, but the thing is old man . . . we just can't afford it.

SCORE

by Lyndon Brook

A tennis net is stretched across stage over the floats. HARRY *and* SHEILA, *in white, hold rackets, but mime the use of tennis balls.*

HARRY (*not pleased*). That's another game to you two . . . (*Lifts his head at some remark from our side of the net.*) Now Jim! Don't you start feeling sorry for us – this is all part of our tactics, we're lulling you into a false sense of superiority!

SHEILA (*collecting balls upstage*). False?

HARRY (*to query from* 'JANE'). Score? Ah yes – (*Clicking his fingers at* SHEILA.) Sheila, what's the score?

SHEILA. Don't you click your fingers at me! We're losing, I can tell that much.

HARRY. Very helpful.

SHEILA. Well, for heaven's sake, you're supposed to be keeping it!

HARRY. Let's see . . . it's your serve —

SHEILA. I know we've won two games —

HARRY. And I started serving this set —

SHEILA. I *think* it's two – five (*She indicates her side and opponents' side of net.*)

HARRY. Hell, really? (*Turns front.*) Know the score, Jim? . . . Two – *four*! . . . No, no. (*Pleased.*) If you say so – we've – er – we've lost count! (*Traps ball from* JIM.) Thanks! (*Traps ball from* JANE *right.*) Grazie (*pronounced Grahtsy-eh*) Jane! Sheila's serve! (*Throws ball back in general direction of* SHEILA.) Put it on his backhand. (*Settles and smiles at* JANE.)

    Slight pause. SHEILA *is getting her hair in place, then collects two balls and comes to base line to serve.*

(*To* JANE.) Sorry, was I staring? . . . Oh! Your hair! I thought you said my –. . . I think it looks wonderful . . . I wish you'd tell

Sheila where you go: she has such a terrible time keeping it even presentable! . . . Oh yes, the hair's all right – it's what she does with it, poor darling.

> SHEILA *serves.* HARRY *misses* JIM'S *return.*

HARRY. Damn! Good shot, Jim! (*To* JANE.) Better keep my eye on the *ball*! (*To* SHEILA.) I said his *back*hand!

SHEILA (*calm*). It was the wind.

HARRY. Oh. (*Then, realising.*) There's not a *breath* of wind!

> *He has crossed down right.* SHEILA *collects balls on way up* left.

SHEILA. Love-fifteen.

> SHEILA *serves. Into the net.* HARRY *picks it up quickly. On* SHEILA'S *second serve* HARRY *misses* JANE'S *sideline return.*

(*Sweetly.*) Wouldn't you be more use back here, darling?

HARRY. Server's partner always stands at the net.

SHEILA. Only when he can make contact with the occasional ball, surely.

> SHEILA *goes right to pick up ball.* HARRY *crosses down left and talks across right to* JANE.

HARRY. Afraid we're not giving you much of a match, Jane . . . Oh, well, if you play every week! . . . No, Sheila always seems to have so much to do – in the house . . . Oh yes, au pairs – they never stay, though.

SHEILA. Love – Thirty.

HARRY. We've a Belgian girl at the moment . . .

SHEILA. You'll get hurt, Harry, if you stand so far over as that!

HARRY (*moving left but continuing talking to* JANE). But I caught *her* looking up the cross-Channel ferries yesterday.

> SHEILA *serves. Into the net.* HARRY *picks up the ball.*

Sheila just can't get on with them.

> SHEILA *serves again. Into net.* HARRY *picks it up.*

Double.

SHEILA (*cutting but smiling*). Yes, I saw.

HARRY (*to* JANE). *I* find them – stimulating. They keep you young!

SHEILA. Balls; please. (*She is up left.*)

> HARRY *bounces the two balls he has in his hand back to her.*
> Love – forty.

>> SHEILA *serves.* HARRY *takes vicious swipe at the return and wins the point.*

HARRY. Grazie, Jim, it wasn't too bad, was it!

SHEILA. Fifteen – forty.

> HARRY *hasn't moved.*

> (*Repeats.*) Fifteen – forty. (*Pause.*) Other side, Harry.

HARRY. Oh. (*Moves left speaks right to* JANE.) That's my best shot – I've been trying to get it back all day!

>> SHEILA *serves. It hits* HARRY *on the neck.*

> Ow!

SHEILA. I warned you – you were practically on the centre line!

HARRY (*to* JANE). I suppose that's what they call a lethal serve.

> HARRY *moves further left.* SHEILA *serves. The return goes to her and she drives to* JANE. HARRY *repeats his swipe and wins the point.*

HARRY. That's better! (*Crossing right.*) *Thirty* – forty! Now, we need a couple more like that —

SHEILA. *I* need something to serve with.

HARRY. Eh? Oh – (*Starts looking for balls.*)

SHEILA (*trapping one and then another from* JIM). Thank you, Jim – (*Low.*) Glad someone has some manners.

HARRY. Oh, stop nagging.

SHEILA. Thirty – forty, then.

> *She serves from up left.* HARRY *takes third swipe, grins delightedly at the result and starts to turn upstage.*

HARRY. Deuce! (*Stops centre and turns to* JIM.) *Out*?! (*Looks at* SHEILA.) Out?! (*Then back at* JIM.) Are you sure, Jim? . . . No, no, I just thought – . . . Oh, thanks, Jane, no, there's no need to play it again – if *you* say . . . (*Slight pause.*) I must admit I thought . . .

SHEILA. Don't argue, Harry.

> HARRY *moves back towards* SHEILA.

Your game, then – (*She hits ball across to* JANE. *Turns to* HARRY.) Five – two.

HARRY. Did it look out to you?

SHEILA. Couldn't possibly tell from back here. I take Jim's word.

HARRY. You would. (*Throws a couple of balls over net from baseline*.) Your serve, Jane.

SHEILA. Don't know what's worrying you. Thought you wanted them to win.

HARRY. What on earth are you talking about?

SHEILA. You said it might make things easier at the office —

HARRY. If we didn't beat them by too wide a margin, you idiot! I never said —

SHEILA. Well, that's not very likely, is it, the way you're playing!

HARRY. And you're Virginia Wade, I suppose! If you're so —

SHEILA. What were you nattering to Jane about?

HARRY. Oh, this and that . . . What Jim? Oh yes, we're ready.

SHEILA. You'd do better to concentrate on the game. Tennis.

HARRY (*to* JIM). Just a little conference on tactics. (*Moves to net left*.) Yes, Jane: – five – two . . . Cinque – due – (*Cheenkweh-Dooeh*.)

SHEILA (*mutters*). Eight days in San Remo . . .

     SHEILA *receives serve. Her return is smashed by* JIM.

HARRY. Shot, Jim! (*To* SHEILA.) You gave it to him on a plate!

SHEILA. Couldn't help it – my racket slipped.

HARRY. That's just your trouble – you don't use the right grip. Your racket can't slip if you hold it properly: like this. (*He demonstrates*.) Look – *you* hold it like *this*!

SHEILA. Who's nagging now? . . . Here you are, Jane! (*Throws ball across and moves down right to net position and talks across to* JIM *left*.) What, Jim? . . . Oh, do you think so? (*Looks down at, smoothes her dress*.) How nice of you to say – . . . Heavens no, I made it myself, from a pattern . . . I'm lucky to be able to buy darning wool on the dress allowance Harry gives me . . . I'm always green with envy at Jane's clothes.

HARRY *receives* JANE'S *serve. His return is smashed by* JIM.
What was that about handing it on a plate?

HARRY. It was Jane's serve. It was a brute! . . . Lovely serve,
Janey!

SHEILA. Janey? Since when Janey?

HARRY. Everyone calls her that.

SHEILA. I don't.

HARRY. Come on – it's thirty – love.

SHEILA, *up right, returns* JANE'S *serve.*
Well done.

HARRY, *at net left, returns next shot,* SHEILA *the next, but
when ball comes back fourth time* HARRY *makes attempt to
stretch across right.*

HARRY. All right, mine! (*Misses it.*) No – yours!

But SHEILA *has changed courts by now and can't retrieve*
HARRY'S *miss.*

SHEILA. Oh charming! I could have got it perfectly well if
you –

HARRY (*becoming more and more tense*). Then why didn't you!

He picks up two balls at baseline and smashes them across net.
SHEILA *walks to position at net right.*

SHEILA. Calm down, darling, it's only a game. (*To* JIM.)
Honestly, I don't know what's the matter with Harry today –
he's right off . . . Yes, he should, you're right . . . It's all I can
do to get him out to post a letter sometimes . . . He comes back
from the office and just slumps in a chair watching television . . .
(*Laughs.*) Oh yes, he always watches Wimbledon . . . you'd
never have guessed it, would you!

HARRY. Sheila! It's forty – love! Match point!

SHEILA. Well, try not to send this one straight to Jimmy –
(*Smiles at* JIM.) He's got a terrific smash.

HARRY. Got a terrific what?

SHEILA (*dry and clipped*). Smash.

HARRY *returns* JANE'S *serve to* JANE. *Ball comes back to*
SHEILA *who plays it to* JIM. JIM *smashes to* HARRY *who,*

wide left, gets it back to JANE. JANE'S *shot comes back very
high and* SHEILA *starts to run backwards.*

All right!

HARRY. *I* can!

*He hopping sideways from left, she hopping backwards from
right, eyes on the high ball, bump and land on their knees. Then
the ball lands on* HARRY'S *head.*

HARRY. Typical! Is there nothing you can do right?!

SHEILA. Oh, Harry – for God's sake —

HARRY. I had a chance at a beautiful shot, so of course I get
knocked out of the way. Hell, Sheila, it's not as if you were
good at anything else – it's the same casual, half-hearted,
sloppy approach to everything that makes you such a mess as a
person!

SHEILA. My approach —

HARRY. It's only a game! Isn't that what you said? Only a game!
So that means you don't have to put anything into it – just slop
along and titter when you make a complete fool of yourself – and
me – (*Turning still full of anger.*) Yes Jim what is it?!

SHEILA. He said it's only a game.

Pause while HARRY *looks at each of them, calms himself, and
musters a smile.*

HARRY. Well, I suppose we should be thankful there are no bones
broken! Well! Game set and match! (*Approaches net.*) Well
played you two!

SHEILA. Beaten fair and square.

HARRY (*to* JANE). Mmm? . . . No, no – please go on, Jane – I'm
always glad to learn from an expert . . . How do you mean, my
grip? . . . Oh yes? . . . Well . . . I must try to remember that
(*Trying it.*) Yes . . . see that, darling?

SHEILA (*mild*). Yes.

HARRY. Thank you, Jane . . .

SHEILA (*to* JIM). No, we're in no hurry, are we, Harry.

HARRY. No . . . Lovely! But I insist on buying them . . . No, Jim,
I insist! . . . No. I'm not going to have you buying —

SHEILA (*interrupts*). Well, the *second* round, then. Come on, Harry, help me collect the balls.

HARRY (*to* JIM *and* JANE). No, you go ahead – we'll be right with you.

> HARRY *moves to help* SHEILA. *They both stop and look after their departing opponents.*

HARRY (*sighing*). I suppose we need more practice.

SHEILA. Intensive training, if you're hoping tennis will help your career.

HARRY. Sorry, darling.

SHEILA. It's all right. There are some behind you. (*He leaves her.*) If only you didn't get so het up!

HARRY. Maybe I should take up bridge – not half as exhausting.

SHEILA. You'd be that much closer to Janey at the card table.

HARRY. You *jealous*?

SHEILA. Oh, now, Harry, darling, please. Even you can't seriously think you'd get anywhere with *that* one. How could I possibly be jealous?

HARRY. Oh.

SHEILA. Besides, you can tell they're both mad about each other.

HARRY. Yes ... I must admit, I see Jim's point! She's quite a girl.

SHEILA. Oh, I never denied that – they're a very handsome couple.

HARRY (*thinking of* JANE). Beautiful.

SHEILA. The trouble is, they *know* it. (*Points.*) There's one over there. And all the time she must spend – to say nothing of money – keeping up that glossy look ... lovely, I know – but is it *worth* it!

HARRY. I imagine Jim thinks so. Of course, he's the brainy one of the two – brilliant at the office, you know. I really wasn't jealous when he was promoted – he deserved it.

SHEILA. He always gives me the feeling of pressure ... that his brain's ticking away ...

HARRY. Yes ... Well, let's face it, you can be too clever, can't you. I mean ... it's brought him a good job and wonderful prospects – but the strain of always keeping one jump ahead – trying to outguess everyone else – I don't think I could live like that.

SHEILA. No . . .

HARRY. That the lot?

SHEILA (*she glances into the box he holds*). Six. Yes.

HARRY. Come along then, Miss Wade . . .

SHEILA. Yes, Mr Laver – or may I call you 'Rod'?

They move downstage to follow JIM *and* JANE.

HARRY (*stops*). Yes . . . they may be attractive, and clever, successful, well-adjusted . . . and happy . . . but don't let's fool ourselves, there's more to life than that, isn't there.

SHEILA *turns to look at him as blackout.*

THE LAWYER

A LAWYER *interviewing an unseen lady plaintiff who intends to divorce her husband. He is middle-aged, formally dressed, but the kind of solicitor usually described as 'sharp' rather than 'old family'. He talks with a plummy legal accent which slips occasionally on the more complicated vowel sounds.*

Yes, yes, yes. I know he's not opposing it at the moment but I know his solicitors, no disrespect to colleagues but they're going to do their best to persuade him that it would be in his best interests to reconsider . . .

. . . Now let's see what we *have* got shall we? There's the man who thought it was the W.C. instead of a mop cupboard, and the char-lady who discovered an intimate garment concealed among the coils of the vacuum cleaner. Useful I agree but not really enough. There's your discretion clauses you see. One . . . well that would be understandable. A single lapse motivated by the emotional shock of discovering his callous infidelity committed in the family home. One yes, but two . . . and one of them with a man who came to adjust the thermostat on the central heating plant. They could make great play with that you see . . .

Snore. Did he snore? . . . Sometimes. Would you say as a side-effect of excessive drinking? Excess . . . excess . . . were his demands what a dutiful wife might consider . . . On the contrary. Dear, dear, dear. I don't think we'll use that. Your average judge isn't favourably impressed by a lady plaintiff who admits to what you might describe as . . . er . . . strong appetites . . . Appetites. Were; his tastes normal? Rubber for instance. Any rubber articles he was prone to? . . . Hot water bottles? . . . No, you don't understand me. I was referring to inflatable masks, plastic under garments, fur? Fancy dress then. Tell me did he ever suggest you grace the marital chamber disguised as a nun, a school-girl, lady astronaut, or circus equestrian . . . Look, madam, I am trying to help . . . Well, if that's the way you feel, we'll just have to rely on the evidence we've got but I don't like it. I don't like it at all. It's too straight up and down for my liking.

NORMA

by Alun Owen

The WOMAN *is seated alone in the shelter in the Park. She is huddled up in a raincoat and stares out into the middle distance. After a few moments she speaks aloud to herself as in answering a question.*

WOMAN. That's all very well but . . . oh no, you couldn't say that, it sounds soft.

MAN (*voice off*). Darling! Darling!

The WOMAN *looks in the direction of the voice then waves and smiles.*

WOMAN. Sod you, Mate!

The MAN *runs into the shelter from the rain, he is excited and happy.*

MAN. I'm terribly sorry.

WOMAN (*looking at him*). You're very wet.

MAN (*shaking himself*). I'd no idea of the time.

WOMAN. Is it warm enough to take your coat off?

MAN (*dabbing his face dry*). And I ran all the way.

WOMAN. Well, you would through all that rain, wouldn't you?

For the first time, the MAN *really notices her.*

MAN (*smiling at her*). Yes, I did.

He sits beside her and takes her hand and speaks with romantic concern.

MAN. Well – how are you?

WOMAN (*moving slightly*). I'd take that coat off if I was you and give it a good shaking.

MAN (*gallantly*). It doesn't matter.

WOMAN (*edgily*). I would have thought it did – it's only shower proof.

MAN. Oh, I don't know.

WOMAN. It is, Roy's got one just like it.

MAN. But this is French.

WOMAN (*primly*). Oddly enough so is Roy's.

MAN. What's the matter?

WOMAN. What do you mean?

MAN. Nothing, just what's the matter?

WOMAN. I don't know what you're talking about.

MAN. Will it be better – I mean, all right, if I take my coat off and shake it?

WOMAN. Well, that's up to you. Summer showers lead to summer colds, the worst sort, they drag on and there's nothing worse than a cold in August. I had one two years ago – ruined the holiday. Roy got it in the end.

MAN (*astonished*). I don't believe it.

WOMAN (*rattling on*). Perfectly true – Fuengirola – both of us with the sniffles in Fuengirola. He was marvellous about it actually considering I gave the wretched cold to him in the first place.

MAN (*quietly*). Shut up!

WOMAN. What?

MAN. I said, 'Shut up', Norma, what's going on?

WOMAN. Nothing's going on, I was just warning you, that's all.

MAN. You were warning me all right but what about though, cos I'm bloody sure it's got nothing to do with this coat but I'll have it off straight away if that's what you want.

WOMAN. That's up to you, I was just . . .

MAN (*interrupting her*). . . . warning me, I know.

> *He takes off the offending coat and gives it a vigorous shaking then turns back to her.*

MAN. Well?

> *She rises.*

WOMAN. Let me stretch it out – oh no, there's a nail thing there. (*She indicates a place.*) If I can hang it up it'll drip down. They dry quite quickly.

C

MAN (*grimly*). Even in the damp?

WOMAN. Yes, the material is specially treated. – Impermeable –
see, it says so on the label.

    He grabs her and kisses her, she is pretty limp. They break.
Somebody's told Roy.

MAN. Oh.

WOMAN. Yeah – oh.

MAN. When did this happen?

WOMAN. Some time last week, I don't know – he didn't eat much
lunch yesterday so I knew there was something up.

    This expression irritates the MAN.

MAN. Up?

WOMAN. Well, wrong – he usually eats a good lunch on Sundays.

MAN. I suppose Roy's eating arrangements *are* important.

WOMAN. In this case, very.

MAN. I would of thought his knowing had the edge on his failure
to gobble down his usual wodge of roast and yorkshire but
you'd know best.

WOMAN (*tartly*). I ought to, I'm married to the man.

    There is a hostile pause.

MAN (*contrite*). I'm sorry, I really am.

WOMAN (*contrite*). I had to tell you in my own way, that's all.

MAN. Of course you did.

WOMAN. He just sat there and looked at it.

MAN. The meal?

WOMAN. Yeah . . . he sighed.

MAN. Sighed?

WOMAN. Yeah, a sort of little sigh.

MAN. And?

WOMAN. He said, 'Ah well' and pushed the plate away. Of course
I knew then something was up – I mean wrong.

MAN. So what did you do?

WOMAN. I cleared the plate away and went into the kitchen, I was
pretty shaken, I can tell you.

MAN. I can see. Did he say anything?

WOMAN. Not then.

MAN. Just gave you the silent treatment?

WOMAN. Yes. Anyway, I went up to bed after I'd washed the dishes.

MAN. What for?

WOMAN. I always wash the dishes so I don't have to face them afterwards.

MAN (*fascinated*). After what?

WOMAN (*matter of fact*). We always go to bed on Sunday afternoons.

MAN. Do you?

WOMAN. Of course – it's one of the few times Roy isn't too tired.

MAN (*echoing*). Too tired?

WOMAN. To make love.

MAN. Oh.

WOMAN. What's the matter?

MAN. Nothing – it's – I didn't think you still —

WOMAN. Made love with Roy? Of course I do, I live with him, I'm married to him.

MAN. All right, don't go on about it! – Well obviously nothing happened yesterday.

WOMAN. Yes it did.

MAN. A row?

WOMAN. Yes, after.

MAN. After?

WOMAN. After we made love.

MAN. Oh.

WOMAN. He was lying there smoking.

MAN. You don't have to draw a picture, you know.

WOMAN. I'm just telling you what happened.

MAN. All right, all right . . . what happened?

WOMAN. He just said, 'You've been committing adultery, haven't you, Norma?'

MAN. Christ!

WOMAN. I was a bit surprised myself, after all, we'd just been . . .

MAN (*stopping her*). Yes, I know, so of course you denied it.

WOMAN. No I didn't, I said, 'Yes, dear'.

MAN. Oh, Peachy!

WOMAN. Well, I was comfy and relaxed and wasn't really thinking.

MAN. Did he make a scene?

WOMAN. No, he got up and sat by the window, looking out.

MAN. What happened next?

WOMAN. I must have dozed off.

MAN. Dozed off!!

WOMAN. Not for long.

MAN. The time is irrelevant, you dozed off.

WOMAN. Well, I was tired, it's been a long week.

MAN. I can't believe it.

WOMAN. He was still sitting by the window – he had his pyjama coat on now. I went over to him. He was staring out at the rain.

MAN. That bloody monsoon out there, you mean.

WOMAN. I touched him on the leg – it was cold. He looked at me as if he was surprised I was there. Then it happened.

MAN. What happened?

WOMAN. He started to cry.

MAN. Playing for sympathy.

WOMAN. He didn't sob or anything, he just cried, the tears just came out and went down his face, it was a bit sad.

MAN. What did you do?

WOMAN. I got him his dressing gown and pyjama trousers, he had his slippers on.

MAN. I mean, what did you say?

WOMAN. Nothing, I couldn't think of anything to say – so I just did things.

MAN. Did you get him a drink?

WOMAN. It was only half past four. I went downstairs and made the tea.

MAN. Just like that.

WOMAN. That's the way it was and I couldn't change it.

MAN. You didn't even try.

WOMAN. Making the tea seemed to be the right thing to do so I made it.

MAN. Did he come down.

WOMAN. I called him and he came – he was dressed. I thought I'd better explain.

MAN. Didn't you ask him how he found out?

WOMAN. No – that didn't seem to matter – well, I'd admitted it so I could hardly go back on it, could I?

MAN. Did he mention me?

WOMAN. No.

MAN. Did you mention me?

WOMAN. No, he wasn't – well, he didn't seem that interested in who it was and it's not as if you know each other.

MAN (*slightly indignant*). Well, I've seen him about.

WOMAN. Oh, he did ask if it was anyone he knew and I think he was glad he didn't know who it was – no – he didn't seem to care who it was once he knew he didn't know him.

MAN. Well, I care.

WOMAN. Why?

MAN. Why? Well, I'm involved too, you know. Was he angry?

WOMAN. He was more hurt, he didn't like looking at me, I felt I'd offended him.

MAN. Well, you have.

WOMAN. But I'd never thought of it like that.

MAN (*accusingly*). You don't sound as if you thought about it at all.

WOMAN. Well all right, I hadn't really.

MAN. Well what were you thinking about then?

WOMAN. It was nice to be with a man who only wanted to please me and play with me. Lots of fun and no responsibilities – like a separate holiday, you must know what I mean?

MAN. Sorry, I don't.

WOMAN. Well, I certainly didn't want to hurt Roy, why should I? I like him.

MAN. But what about me?

WOMAN. You? – Oh, well, you've enjoyed it, haven't you?

MAN. Sure but I love you.

WOMAN. Does that mean you stop enjoying it?

MAN. No but it means it's a bit more serious than you are making it sound.

WOMAN. But I've got serious at home – I just wanted fun.

MAN. God, I thought I meant a little more to you than fun.

WOMAN. Why are you knocking fun? Fun was what I hadn't got and for the past two months you've been giving me what I hadn't got, I'm very grateful.

MAN. My pleasure.

WOMAN. I hope so – but it's got to stop.

MAN. What!

WOMAN. Oh yes, it's got to stop.

MAN. Why?

WOMAN. Roy said it aloud, now I can see it.

MAN. What?

WOMAN. Adultery.

MAN. But you said it was fun.

WOMAN. Not for Roy.

MAN. Well, he better make his own arrangements.

WOMAN. No, you don't understand, I didn't mean to hurt him.

MAN. What about me?

WOMAN. No, it's Roy I've got to think about.

MAN. Why, suddenly why have you got to think about him?

WOMAN. Cos he doesn't like it.

MAN. What's 'it'? – go on, define 'it'.

WOMAN. My doing adultery with you – it hurts him and anything that hurts people is wrong.

MAN. I'll be hurt if you stop.

WOMAN. Yes, I'm sorry but then I'm married to Roy.

MAN. But don't I mean anything to you?

WOMAN. Of course you do, you're fun and you made me happy all the time I was with you but Roy's real.

MAN. And I'm not. I'm just fun.

WOMAN. Yes. We enjoy saying we love each other but we don't mean it, we . . .

MAN (*interrupting her*). I mean it.

WOMAN. I'm glad you think you do. No, you see, I've got too much time on my hands, it's been the same ever since the kids went to school and we could afford a daily. I kept on getting bored and restless and Roy was tired. Well, I can't do much other than being a girl and I found myself getting langourous.

MAN. Langourous?

WOMAN. Yes – like in the afternoons and Roy's so busy expanding the business I wanted someone to help me.

MAN. God, you don't half choose the wrong words – you were using me.

WOMAN. Was I, I hadn't thought that much about it. I couldn't make do with books and stuff so when we met – I loved you following me, I loved that most, the way you followed me every afternoon, it was terrible.

MAN. What was terrible about it, you attracted me.

WOMAN. Oh, I know that but it was delicious, it excited me, but I was being selfish so I've got to stop it.

MAN. And it hasn't occurred to you you're being selfish now. What about me?

WOMAN. You haven't cried. I knew it was wrong when Roy cried – he's not the sort to cry and when he did, I knew I'd hurt him, I told him I only did it to feel a bit more alive. He said, 'But you have to go so near to someone to do it'. That's what hurt him most, he likes me near him, he thinks being near is very important. I think he's probably right so good-bye. I've got to get home for tea.

> *She runs off quickly into the rain, leaving the man. It takes him a moment before he realises what has happened then he shouts after her.*

MAN. Norma! Norma! Norma!

THE NANNIE

The NANNIE, *a traditional* NANNIE, *in her late fifties, is sitting on a park bench talking to her imaginary friend and rocking her pram. The* NANNIE *talks in a refined cockney.*

I'm not saying we didn't enjoy it. I'm not saying it wasn't value for money, but I wouldn't want to go again. It was the shopping you see, the shopping wasn't a patch on Instanbool. Not that I'd want to go to Instanbool again next year. Nannie said to me 'Nannie' she said 'I wouldn't want to go to Instanbool, not next year anyway'. So we haven't really decided but we do know it won't be Tanjeers again. We'd never want to go there again, not that it wasn't nice and the food was very nice. The food was nicer that Instanbool, and ample helpings, but the shopping was very inadequate. I bought little Peregrine (*she looks into the pram*) a leather camel. It came to pieces within the week. Well . . . and quite expensive. Quite expensive it was. No. Tanjeers no . . .

A pause. She rocks the pram.

Nannie's keen on Tunis-ea, but I'm not keen. I'm not that keen on North Africa, not after Tanjeers. It's the wind. The wind can be quite tiring and there's the flies. We had to change our room. It was at the front of the hotel you see, under the palm trees. The flies come from them you see. Of course there is the cream. You can rub on the cream. That keeps off the flies but you can't spend your whole holiday rubbing on cream. It takes up all the time. There's no time for the shopping if you're rubbing on the cream. Not that the shopping was nice. Not in Tanjeers.

A pause. She rocks the pram.

But I do agree with Nannie about one thing, and she agrees with me. 'Nannie' she said only yesterday, by the round pond it was, 'Nannie' she said. 'Yes Nannie' I said. 'We got to go somewhere we haven't been before. You don't want to go to the same place twice' she says, 'It's so boring'.

NIGHT

by Harold Pinter

A WOMAN *and* MAN *in their forties.*
They sit with coffee.

MAN. I'm talking about that time by the river.

WOMAN. What time?

MAN. The first time. On the bridge. Starting on the bridge.

Pause.

WOMAN. I can't remember.

MAN. On the bridge. We stopped and looked down at the river. It was night. There were lamps lit on the towpath. We were alone. We looked up the river. I put my hand on the small of your waist. Don't you remember? I put my hand under your coat.

Pause.

WOMAN. Was it winter?

MAN. Of course it was winter. It was when we met. It was our first walk. You must remember that.

WOMAN. I remember walking. I remember walking with you.

MAN. The first time? Our first walk?

WOMAN. Yes, of course I remember that.

Pause.

WOMAN. We walked down a road into a field, through some railings. We walked to a corner of the field and then we stood by the railings.

MAN. No. It was on the bridge that we stopped.

Pause.

WOMAN. That was someone else.

MAN. Rubbish.

WOMAN. That was another girl.

MAN. It was years ago. You've forgotten.

Pause.

MAN. I remember the light on the water.

WOMAN. You took my face in your hands, standing by the railings. You were very gentle, you were very caring. You cared. Your eyes searched my face. I wondered who you were. I wondered what you thought. I wondered what you would do.

MAN. You agree we met at a party. You agree with that?

WOMAN. What was that?

MAN. What?

WOMAN. I thought I heard a child crying.

MAN. There was no sound.

WOMAN. I thought it was a child, crying, waking up.

MAN. The house is silent.

Pause.

It's very late. We're sitting here. We should be in bed. I have to be up early. I have things to do. Why do you argue?

WOMAN. I don't. I'm not. I'm willing to go to bed. I have things to do. I have to be up in the morning.

Pause.

MAN. A man called Doughty gave the party. You knew him, I had met him. I knew his wife. I met you there. You were standing by the window. I smiled at you, and to my surprise you smiled back. You liked me. I was amazed. You found me attractive. Later you told me. You liked my eyes.

WOMAN. You liked mine.

Pause.

WOMAN. You touched my hand. You asked me who I was, and what I was, and whether I was aware that you were touching my hand, that your fingers were touching mine, that your fingers were moving up and down between mine.

MAN. No. We stopped on a bridge. I stood behind you. I put my hand under your coat, onto your waist. You felt my hand on you.

Pause.

WOMAN. We had been to a party. Given by the Doughtys. You

had known his wife. She looked at you dearly, as if to say you were her dear. She seemed to love you. I didn't. I didn't know you. They had a lovely house. By a river. I went to collect my coat, leaving you waiting for me. You had offered to escort me. I thought you were quite courtly, quite courteous, pleasantly mannered, quite caring. I slipped my coat on and looked out of the window, knowing you were waiting. I looked down over the garden to the river, and saw the lamplight on the water. Then I joined you and we walked down the road through railings into a field, must have been some kind of park. Later we found your car. You drove me.

Pause.

MAN. I touched your breasts.

WOMAN. Where?

MAN. On the bridge. I felt your breasts.

WOMAN. Really?

MAN. Standing behind you.

WOMAN. I wondered whether you would, whether you wanted to, whether you would.

MAN. Yes.

WOMAN. I wondered how you would go about it, whether you wanted to, sufficiently.

MAN. I put my hands under your sweater, I undid your brassière, I felt your breasts.

WOMAN. Another night perhaps. Another girl.

MAN. You don't remember my fingers on your skin?

WOMAN. Were they in your hands? My breasts? Fully in your hands?

MAN. You don't remember my hands on your skin?

Pause.

WOMAN. Standing behind me?

MAN. Yes.

WOMAN. But my back was against railings. I felt the railings . . . behind me. You were facing me. I was looking into your eyes. My coat was closed. It was cold.

MAN. I undid your coat.

WOMAN. It was very late. Chilly.

MAN. And then we left the bridge and we walked down the towpath and we came to a rubbish dump.

WOMAN. And you had me and you told me you had fallen in love with me, and you said you would take care of me always, and you told me my voice and my eyes, my thighs, my breasts, were incomparable, and that you would adore me always.

MAN. Yes I did.

WOMAN. And you do adore me always.

MAN. Yes I do.

WOMAN. And then we had children and we sat and talked and you remembered women on bridges and towpaths and rubbish dumps.

MAN. And you remembered your bottom against railings and men holding your hands and men looking into your eyes.

WOMAN. And talking to me softly.

MAN. And your soft voice. Talking to them softly at night.

WOMAN. And they said I will adore you always.

MAN. Saying I will adore you always.

Part Two

THE PSYCHOANALYST

The PSYCHOANALYST *is middle-aged, foreign and very neatly dressed. He sits in a chair facing the head of the couch on which his* PATIENT *is lying unseen.*

The pauses between what he says, should, while of variable length, be as long as an audience can bear and at the same time it should be clear, from his reactions, that his patient says nothing.

What are you sinking or am I interrupting? (*Pause.*) I'm going to suggest that that is a very aggressive reaction, and I am wondering if today your aggression is connecting eventually wiz ze cheque you put on my desk when you came in? Why aren't you putting it me in the hand? Do you feel it is abusing me to pay up? . . . .

. . . .
. . . . I would like here to bring in the dream you spoke of earlier . . . . You went to a garden shed to fetch some shears and discovered yourself employed in a brothel of the old style and being given a hundred guineas to buy yourself a car . . . .

. . . .
May I suggest an interpretation. The shears are to cut me off from you in effect. A very aggressive idea . . . . and you'll acknowledge that the hundred guineas is the same as your monthly bill for your analysis . . . . Of course the shears may work on another level, to castrate me so as you can the better identify wiz me . . . . and the car is for you to get here more easily than wiz a bus or taxi . . . . How is this fitting? . . . . . Yet again you reject my interpretation . . . . You know, analysis is like walking down a long corridor. I can propose to open doors for you, but only you can say if they are the right doors. But if I am to help you, you must verbalise. How else can I know what you are really feeling against me? . . . (*He looks at his*

watch.) Your time is up now . . . . (*He watches her get up off the couch.*) . . . . . I'll see you tomorrow at the same hour.

The off-stage door bangs. He takes cheque out of envelope, and looks at it.

She's done it again – pounds!

PERMANENCE

by Fay Weldon

A MAN *and a* WOMAN *sit in a tent. The* MAN *reads, the* WOMAN *doesn't. He speaks absently. She doesn't. She is very attractive though forty.*

HELEN. Peter.

PETER. Yes.

HELEN. It's raining.

PETER. I know.

HELEN. When it rains and you're in a tent, there's a kind of orange glow. It's a very soft light, and very pretty. It used to be like that in church when I was a child, through the stained glass windows. I never remembered that until now. It's one of the things I look forward to about camping, every year, the way the light falls in this tent. Did you know that? In town when it rains, it just rains. When you're camping, it's important. It seems the most important thing about the whole day, the rain; and of course, you see it is. One tends to forget about nature.

PETER. Does one?

HELEN. What are you reading?

PETER. A book.

HELEN. A pity I lost my glasses.

PETER. You didn't lose them, you broke them.

HELEN. Well they are lost to me I mean. All those books, and I can't read any of them. I've never had a holiday before without reading. Silly sort of accident wasn't it?

PETER. There's no such thing as an accident.

HELEN. What do you mean?

PETER. You must have wanted to break your glasses, or you

wouldn't have jumped on them. Don't ask me why, I don't
know the way your mind works.

HELEN. Peter, I did not want to be stung by that wasp. There is
no one in the world wants to be stung by a wasp. Not even me.

PETER. If you didn't want to be stung by a wasp you wouldn't
have leant against it.

HELEN. But I didn't know it was there.

PETER. You must have heard it buzzing. If only subconsciously.

HELEN. Oh. Do you think so? It still hurts. Poor wasp. I didn't
mean to kill it.

PETER. But you did.

HELEN. Well you know how it is. Something hurts you and you
lash out.

PETER. I know very well.

HELEN. Anyway, I broke my glasses, so that's me served right.

PETER. Tell that to the wasp, I'm sure it'll be very impressed.

HELEN. Well whatever it is you're reading, it doesn't make you
very sympathetic.

PETER (*putting his book down for one minute, but one minute only*).
How old are you?

HELEN. The same age as you. Forty; young for a man, old for a
woman. Why?

PETER. Sometimes you talk as if you were six.

HELEN. Oh. I thought perhaps you were going to say you don't
look forty, you look twenty, or something nice. You never say
anything nice, only hard truths.

PETER. The only point in being alive is to find out the truth.

HELEN. That's why you're a historian I suppose. What if the
truth is too horrible to bear?

PETER (*back to his book*). I'm trying to read, Helen.

HELEN. Well it's very boring sitting here in a tent, in the rain, not
able to read because a wasp stung you and you jumped a foot
in the air and landed on your glasses.

PETER. You usually like it in the tent when it rains.

HELEN. Things seem a little different this year.

PETER. Oh?

HELEN. I'm forty. Look at my arm. When I bend it, it wrinkles.

PETER. Well of course it does. You've bent it.

HELEN. It wrinkles in a different way than it ever has before. I'm drying up, Peter. When I go brown, I look older instead of younger. And when the air-bed goes down in the middle of the night, I ache in the morning. I never used to. And when I crawl into this tent, I can hardly straighten up. If we had a frame tent, the way everyone else does . . .

PETER. You should do exercises. There's nothing wrong with the tent. It's done us very well.

HELEN. Yes, I'm fond of it actually. And if we had one of the new ones, they're blue mostly. A hard sort of blue. It would take a long time getting used to. I'm not as good at change as I used to be. When it rained there'd be a bluish light, not an orange one.

PETER. What's wrong with a bluish light?

HELEN. It's not very kind to the complexion.

PETER. You've got a very good complexion.

HELEN. It's wrinkling a bit around the eyes, all the same.

PETER. You're getting older. It will.

HELEN. Do you mind?

PETER. Why should I mind?

HELEN. Well, you never know. You've been very keen on all this camping and swimming and sunbathing. Haven't you? Ever since Judy was born. It's not really me, you know. I mean I've adjusted, but as I get older I may well revert to type, and ask for feather cushions in the small of my back. I wouldn't want it to annoy you. I think, you see, you think being young is very important, especially in a woman.

PETER. How do you know what I think? That is my business. Don't interfere!

HELEN. You always say that. Of course I know what you think. We're married.

PETER. Quite so. But we're still two people. At least I hope to God we are.

HELEN (*sad*). Yes. All the same I wouldn't be much good without you. Like a table tennis set with only one bat. Only good for throwing out.

PETER. I wish you hadn't broken your glasses. Why didn't you bring a spare pair? Stop upsetting yourself and let me get on with my book. (*All the same he puts an arm round her as he reads.*)

HELEN. I hope Judy's all right. Supposing she takes to drugs or something while we're away?

PETER. Why should she?

HELEN. We've never had a holiday without Judy before. Do you know what she said, I didn't like to tell you, I thought you'd be annoyed. She said people will think I'm very dull if I go camping with my parents. I said but all your friends go away with their parents, still don't they, and she said, yes, but not camping. Camping! In that funny old tent you have to crawl into, she said.

Still he doesn't react.

Peter, do I seem very dull to you? You never talk to me any more. Peter, what do you want?

PETER, Want? I don't want anything.

HELEN. I'm going to die soon.

PETER. If the wasp sting was going to kill you, it would have done so by now. Stop fussing.

HELEN. I wasn't talking about wasps.

PETER. What then?

HELEN. I'm forty. Forty more years I'll be eighty. Then I'll be dead. It's such a short time. The first half went like a flash. What are we going to do?

PETER. I don't understand your desire to talk things over. Words don't alter what has been. They don't make any difference of what is going to happen. What counts is what you do, not what you say about what you do.

HELEN. I'm sure you're right but it's nothing to do with what I'm saying. You're going to be dead soon, too.

PETER. Thank you very much.

HELEN. It's all this not reading you see. I've been thinking. When you're very young, you get by on going to bed, and all that. Then there's the child and you stay together because it makes links to chain you, and if you so much as try and stretch them, you tear yourself to pieces – but after that —

PETER. I think it's stopped raining. Shall we go and meet the fishing boats and buy some fresh sardines?

HELEN. It's raining just as hard as it ever was.

PETER. You haven't looked.

HELEN. I can tell by the sound. I've spent every summer for the last eighteen years in this tent and I know when it's raining and when it's not. Anyway, fish oil makes everything so smelly. And it always spills.

PETER. Throw it away. You don't have to keep it.

HELEN. I don't like waste. Anyway I don't like cutting off their heads.

PETER. I'll do it.

HELEN. You always say that but you never do. Their little eyes looking at you. I don't know how you ate those quails last night, crunching up their little feet. I was trying to say something important —

PETER. Oh yes. So you were. You were saying you were tired of me and wanted a change.

HELEN. Oh Peter. I was not. I don't want to leave you. I just thought, just possibly, you wanted to leave me, but didn't have the courage to say so.

PETER. Who for?

HELEN. I don't know. Someone younger and prettier, I suppose, who doesn't embarrass you by saying what they feel all the time.

PETER. You don't know what you feel. It's one thing one day and another the next. If you're bored, why don't you write some postcards?

HELEN. I don't want to keep you if you don't want to stay. I'll be all right.

PETER. But you were just saying you wouldn't be any good without me. Like a tennis set with only one racquet.

HELEN. Table tennis with only one bat. Was I? But that has nothing to do with what I'm saying now.

PETER. Oh hasn't it? I rather thought it had. The preamble, as it were. What *are* you saying now?

HELEN. Stop trying to confuse me.

PETER. I'm not trying to confuse you. I'm trying to read a book.

HELEN. You have no poetry in you. I was offering you your freedom, because you're young, and I'm old.

PETER. I'm perfectly free as I am thank you. As I'm sure you are. I think you ought to go on the stage. You're wasted on me.

HELEN. All I'm trying to say is, I know I'm awful. I don't think I'm good enough for you.

PETER. Well I think I'm good enough for you or I wouldn't be sitting here putting up with all this.

HELEN. You were so good about Judy and everything.

PETER. Here we go.

HELEN. Well I mean. I do *think* she's yours. She does like you. She certainly behaves like you a lot of the time. She's very difficult.

PETER. Do just let things be, Helen.

HELEN. It must be very trying for you, I do realize that, never to be able to know. Especially being a historian. On the other hand, perhaps that's why you became one. Because of Judy.

PETER. Please.

HELEN. If you hadn't gone away and left me I would never have done it.

PETER. I'm not blaming you. I never have.

HELEN. But you do. You didn't go away, I know. You were sent away. It just didn't feel like that at the time. I was hurt and angry.

PETER. It's eighteen years ago.

HELEN. I want to make amends.

PETER. No you don't. You just want to talk about it.

HELEN. I hurt you then, didn't I, and our marriage. I killed it, didn't I, like that wasp.

PETER. Is that what you want to believe?

HELEN. No.

PETER. Then why say it? You're sitting there, I'm sitting here. We're together, aren't we?

HELEN. No. Why didn't you want any more children? Just Judy. I mean *really*.

PETER. I didn't think you could cope with any more.

HELEN. Didn't you want more? Of your own?

PETER. Yes.

HELEN. You were punishing me then.

PETER. What do you mean?

HELEN. Cutting off your nose to spite my face.

PETER. What are you trying to make me say? If I'm going to leave you, you want to know now, before you're too old to find anyone else? Is that it?

HELEN. How can you! How can you! You know what I want you to say, and you won't say it, you won't. Will you ever, though you do. You do. I know you do. You love me.

It is a long shriek but he doesn't react. She quietens.

(*Presently.*) Stop being so cruel to me. Just because you know how.

PETER. You always drive me into saying things I don't mean. If for once we're floating on a nice quiet sea, you get your broomstick and stir it until we're all sea-sick.

HELEN (*and she is*). I'm sorry.

PETER. That's all right. I'm used to it. Just sometimes you rock the boat a bit too hard.

HELEN. I could have another baby, still.

PETER. What, and start it all over again?

HELEN. Yes.

PETER. Good God.

HELEN. Well?

PETER. We'll see what happens. You might be right, perhaps

next year we shouldn't go camping. I get backache too. We could take a villa and be more comfortable. Now Judy's leaving home, there's no reason not to be, I suppose. Somewhere down the Italian coast, unless it's too hot for you. Bring me the maps.

HELEN. Oh. That's nice. I'd be sorry to abandon this tent, all the same. I did complain, but I really rather like it, Peter.

PETER. So did I. On and off. (*Presently*.) It's how I spent my youth.

As the lights fade to blackout; the sound of rain is brought up. The tent is struck, and the lights then fade up on the debate area once more.

THE DOCTOR

The DOCTOR *is very brisk. He talks very, very fast. He sits at a desk on which is a decanter of water, some papers and a prescription pad. There is a buzzer through to the waiting room. In front of the desk is a chair on which the (invisible) patients sit. Their entrance and exit could be made more palpable by a door opening and closing off stage at the appropriate moments.*

(*Stubbing out cigarette.*) Well, try to cut down on your smoking, Mr Taylor. I'm going to give you some Lethe-drene. Take one any time you're feeling grumpy and you'll probably find the old pains will just pack their bags and decamp. Yes, yes, good-morning.

Same buzzer and doors routine.

Ah, Miss Jennings. Sit down. You're getting to be a jolly big girl and a jolly pretty girl too. It seems no time since you bit my finger to the bone when I was exploring your tonsils . . . Don't cry. Forgiven you ages ago ha ha . . . (*A pause.*) . . . Now then what seems to be the matter? . . . Are you sure? Well, you'd better leave a specimen with my secretary on your way out. How have your parents taken it? . . . Yes, I dare say, but then your father is senior Church Warden. Do you know who the er . . . (*A pause.*) . . . your mother won't like that will she. She's a very conventional woman. Now stop your blubbing . . . (*He scribbles a prescription.*) I'm going to give you some Optimene, three a day and you'll find yourself actually looking forward to having it. Are you the last . . . ha ha I don't want to get into trouble in the consulting room? . . . (*A pause.*) . . . Splendid. Come and see me again when we know the result of the test . . . Yes yes that's all right . . .

The DOCTOR *presses the buzzer and after a suitable pause (door opens and shuts) he looks up from his papers and indicates the chair.*

Mrs er Hawkins. Do sit down. What's the trouble . . . (*Pause.*) . . . depression. Can't cope? Can't get through the house-work, that sort of thing . . . Yes (*A slight pause.*) Tell me, Mrs Hawkins, how old are you? There's no need to be coy. I am a doctor . . . (*A pause.*) . . . You see, it's what we medical men call 'the menopause' but to the layman or more usually the laywoman the change of life. Mind you I often think it's because your lives don't change enough ha ha. Now not to worry . . . (*He scribbles on his prescription.*) I'm going to give you some Ambrosium. You take three a day, more if necessary, and you'll feel everything's jolly worthwhile. You'll get through the housework like greased lightning. (*Hands imaginary form.*) Come back for more when you've swallowed these.

Head back in papers. Finger rings buzzer. Door closes. Opens. Closes. He looks up. A pause. The door shuts. The DOCTOR *suddenly looks tired. He opens his desk gets out a bottle of multicoloured pills, pours out a handful and swallows them with a glass of water.*

COUNTDOWN

by *Alan Ayckbourn*

The scene takes place after supper, any evening of any week in any year of this twenty-year old marriage.

(NOTE: *The dialogue is mainly spoken thoughts. The actual conversation is printed in italics.*)

HUSBAND *(whistles softly to himself, then murmuring)*. Mmmmmm mmmmm, gnmmmmmmm . . . ah . . . nmmmmmm *(He begins to wrestle with the paper.)* Page one . . . page four . . . Where's page five then? Continued on page five it says. Where is it? They haven't given me a page five . . . Oh yes, it's on the back of page six . . . oh yes . . . this can't be page five . . . it's a sports page. It must be page six, unless I've got two page fours. Where's page four then? Why can't they print the paper the right way round? Ah . . . here we are. Now then. Oh I've forgotten what it was I was reading now. *(He looks towards the door.)* Where's she gone? Making the tea. I haven't heard the whistle. I'll have to get up and carry the tray in when I hear the whistle. I don't know why I ever offered to start carrying the thing in the first place.

I've been carrying trays in and out of the door ever since. If they were heavy I'd understand it. I do nothing except walk from here to the kitchen, from the kitchen to here with that tray. It's empty most of the time anyway. Still I suppose it's a nice gesture. At least I do it every day. Not just when we have visitors. That's when it gets low. That's when it gets sneaky. I know some men who do that. Old Evans does that. Holds the door open for his wife, just because we're there. We know damn well he goes back to slamming it in her face the minute we've gone home. Oh yes we know all about Bert

Evans. Held her chair for her the last time we were there. Took her so much by surprise she nearly fell on the floor. Ha, that tea must be ready by now. Haven't heard the whistle. If she's left that whistle off the kettle it'll be the first time . . . *(Rising.)* And she talks about me leaving the whistle off. *(He goes out.)*

Pause. The WIFE *enters carrying the tray.*

WIFE. What's happened to him this evening? Must be a world crisis if he's actually forgotten to come padding out to carry this tray. Perhaps he's finally given it up. Thank heavens for that. Forever running in and out with this tray. Why doesn't he behave like a man? I'd like to know what he's done with the whistle off that kettle. Where is he then? *(She begins pouring the tea.)*

He re-enters.

HUSBAND. Oh there she is. *(Loudly.) Oh there you are, dear.*

WIFE. What does one say to that? *(Loudly.) Here I am.*

HUSBAND. *Good.* That's a nasty piece of sarcasm if ever I heard one.

WIFE. *Tea.*

HUSBAND. *Oh, tea! That's nice. (He takes cup from her.)*

WIFE. Surprise, surprise . . .

HUSBAND. The way she hands me that tea, you'd think it was a cheque for a hundred pounds. I bet she hid that whistle on purpose. So I wouldn't hear her come out, so she can accuse me of inconsideration . . . I'm tired. I'm really tired· If she wasn't here . . . I'd a good mind to . . . I'm so tired. Dog tired. Flaked out. If she wasn't here . . . I'd be tempted to yawn. But since she is here . . . Can't have her see me yawning. I'll have to swallow the thing and risk giving myself wind.

WIFE. His eyes are watering. It's that small print. I knew he needed glasses. If he wasn't so vain.

He starts to stir his tea.

Go on, go on stir away. I've had three cups by the time he's finished stirring his first. I wouldn't mind if he'd remembered to put sugar in it. And if he expects me to sugar it for him, just so he can complain it's too sweet . . . I'm so tired . . .

HUSBAND. Had an extraordinary dream the other night about a motor mower. Whatever made me? We don't even own a motor mower. No grass. Except for that bit at the side. I suppose that counts as grass. What there is of it. You could cut that with the nail scissors, there's so little of it. Except that I don't think we've got any nail scissors either. I couldn't find them last night for my toe nails. They were catching in the sheet. Serve her right if I'd torn it. She should put things back . . . bathroom cabinet, second shelf. I put the screw eye in there especially. Then she goes and hangs her sponge bag on it instead, so that the door won't shut, so the mirror's at the wrong angle, so I have to shave with one foot in the bath . . . I bet she hasn't put any sugar in this . . .

WIFE. *It's not sugared.*

HUSBAND. *Oh no?* Thank you very much. Calmly watches me spraining my wrist stirring the thing . . .

WIFE. That'll teach him . . . but maybe I should have told him sooner, now I've got to sit through a second performance.

HUSBAND *(laughing loudly). Hey! Do you know what's in the sugar basin . . . the whistle, the whistle off the kettle!*

WIFE *(laughing). Oh really? Fancy. How silly of me.*

HUSBAND. *Silly you!*

They both laugh gaily at some length.

Oh dear.

WIFE. *Oh dear.*

HUSBAND. How stupid can you get?

WIFE. That's made his evening. Well, as long as he doesn't start reading his paper to me.

The HUSBAND *laughs at something he's reading.*

Ah, we've got to the cartoons already. That laugh's for my benefit. I'm supposed to ask him what it's about; well I'm not going to . . .

HUSBAND. This laugh'll keep her in suspense. She's dying to know what it is. Well let her wait . . . *(He laughs again.)*

WIFE. I know. *(She laughs suddenly.)*

HUSBAND. What's she laughing at? She's waiting for me to ask, isn't she? Well I'm not going to.

WIFE. I must try and keep my eyes open.

HUSBAND. Man here pushed his wife under a bus. I'll make sure she reads that.

WIFE. Why's my husband such an old man? He's always been old. When he was young he was old.

The HUSBAND *folds his newspaper.*

Oh no . . . I know what that means . . .

HUSBAND. Oh well, here we go . . . conversation time. *How's the boiler been today?*

WIFE. If he tells me I choked up the air vent with coke, I shall bring a shovel full . . . right into this room, and I shall . . . *No trouble at all today.*

HUSBAND. *Good, must have learnt to behave itself at last, eh? (He chuckles.)*

She laughs.

Oh very funny. Ought to be on the music halls I should.

WIFE. What a man. Not only does he make the worst jokes I've ever heard, he makes the same ones . . .

HUSBAND. *You see, if you keep the air vent unclogged, you're all right.*

WIFE. *So it said in the instructions.*

HUSBAND. I thought we'd get back to that. She's flinging that book of instructions in my face again. I tell her something I know for a fact and what does she do . . . take my word for it? Not on your life.

WIFE. When did I last laugh? I mean really laugh? I do believe it was at our wedding reception . . . Something he must have said. What did he say? What could he have said . . . how did he make me laugh?

HUSBAND. That cycling tour we had. What a good time that

was. Rained every day too. We didn't care . . . We had some laughs. That's what it was, she used to laugh a lot.

WIFE. *The instruction book also says that we shouldn't overfill it with coke . . . either. That might have been the trouble.*

HUSBAND. *Possibly.* She's got coke on the brain . . . that woman. Looks like a bit of coke. Dehydrated. All the goodness sucked out of her. Supposing I . . . supposing I was to make her laugh. Would it help? Tell her a joke, if only she'd smile properly I think I could almost put up with her. Oh, that miserable face. If only I could make her laugh.

WIFE. He's looking very animated this evening. It's finding that whistle. One little thing like that to hold over me just makes his evening. And when I spilt tea on the new table the other morning, he was so delighted. What did he say? 'Trust you'. As though I went round regularly pouring scalding tea on the veneer.

HUSBAND. *That little business of the sugar basin . . . reminds me . . . of something rather amusing . . . a little story . . .*

WIFE. Hello, what's he up to . . . a little story? He's certainly rubbing it in isn't he? *What's that, dear?*

HUSBAND. *It's nothing really . . . rather silly . . .*

WIFE. Bound to be.

HUSBAND. I've done it now. I'm up to my neck in it. What on earth made me do this. I must be mad.

WIFE. *What is it?* Let's get it over with.

HUSBAND. *It's about two people in a café . . . and one of them is talking about people's funny habits, you see . . . he's saying that everyone is slightly odd in some way or other . . . You see . . . And this other chap says 'not everyone at all. I've nothing peculiar about me. I'm completely normal you see.'*

WIFE. Oh, I can see where this is going.

HUSBAND. *Anyway this first bloke says 'oh no, you're as bad as the rest'. And the other bloke says 'how?'*

WIFE. Or do I think he's just telling me a joke. Why's he doing this.

HUSBAND. *Are you listening?*

WIFE. *Yes, dear?*

HUSBAND. *So the bloke says, 'Well now, I've just observed that you just stirred your tea with your right hand . . . '*

WIFE. Why do people tell jokes? To make other people laugh. Why does he want to make me laugh? Does he really want to make me laugh? He must do. It's the only explanation. He *wants* me to laugh.

HUSBAND. *'Yes,' said the bloke. 'Well, that's your peculiarity' said the other bloke. 'Most people use a spoon.'*

WIFE. Just like he used to. He used to walk me home and father said we were peculiar because we just used to stand outside and laugh . . . well most of the time . . . and then we married, and . . . and now it's amazing . . . I think he really wants to . . . he wants to. *Yes, dear, go on, I'm listening.*

HUSBAND. *I've finished.*

WIFE. *Oh.*

HUSBAND. *Not really very funny. I think I'll just take a look at that boiler . . . just to make sure. (He exits.)*

WIFE *(slowly).* You'll find the instructions on the window ledge.

The lights on the central acting area fade to blackout as the sounds of Victor Sylvester are heard once more.

THE UNION OFFICIAL

At the head of a conference table sits a UNION LEADER *arguing the toss with some invisible bosses. He is very tough and aggressive.*
Totally unacceptable! If that's the best you can offer we might as well jack it in now. Don't look so 'opeful, I know that'd suit you down to the ground – *(In a false posh voice.)* 'Despite every effort to reach an agreement.' *(In his ordinary voice.)* I know you lot. But I'm 'ere to reach an agreement for my members, and I'm prepared to sit 'ere all night if necessary. It's not us what's being obstructive. Now, my offer –
Phone rings. Pause.
For me? Thanks . . .
Reaches out. Takes phone.
(Briskly.) Yes? *(His voice changes.)* Oh, it's you dear . . . The thing is it's rather a . . . Yes, but . . . Yes, I've got all your sizes written on the back of my union card, but . . . Yes, dear, if I can. Peach, you say. What if they 'aven't got 'em in peach? . . . Yes, dear, I'm with you, powder blue. It'll depend on whether the shops are still open, but . . .
Hands phone back. Click as it's replaced.
(Less aggressively.) Sorry about that . . . Now don't think we're against a committee to study the redundancy question; it was us pushed for it in the first place, but what we demand is some form of guaranty that . . .
Phone rings again. Pause. He takes it.
Look, dear, I told you that . . . Well, that's very naughty of 'er . . . I know I did, but – oh, all right, put 'er on . . . 'Ullo Linda, now Daddy's very busy . . . I know I said I'd be 'ome to read you a story but Daddy can't always keep 'is promises because sometimes 'is job . . . Of course 'e loves Linda more than 'is union members, but . . . *(Loses temper.)* Look go to bed and shut that bleedin' row.

E

Holds phone and continues more aggressively to the bosses.

Now 'ere's out final conditions: You set up a committee and in the interim we demand an absolute guaranty that no paid-up member will be declared redundant under any . . .

Squawk from phone. He puts it to his ear.

Yes! . . . No dear, I didn't shout at 'er . . . Well, per'aps I did raise my voice, but . . . Of course I love 'er. It's just that . . . And you, dear, of course I do . . . What gave you that idea? . . . Look dear, you kiss Linda and tell 'er Daddy's very sorry 'e shouted at 'er and 'e'll come up an kiss 'er goodnight as soon as 'e comes in . . . Right, dear. Yes . . .

Hands phone back. Click as it's replaced.

(Defeatedly, almost abjectly.) Now, gents, what do you suggest we do. I don't want to be unreasonable, all I ask is to be able to go back to 'eadquarters with some concession 'owever small . . . No? . . . Any chance of another meeting? . . . Well, if you change your mind you know where to find me.

SILVER WEDDING

by John Bowen

A kitchen in a semi-detached house in Purley. It is 8 o'clock. As the clock in the hall strikes, AUDREY *is discovered sitting at the table. As she checks the time with her watch, there is the sound of a key turning in the front door.*

> JULIAN *enters.*

AUDREY. Do you want some tea?

JULIAN. I'm sorry I'm late.

AUDREY. There's plenty in the pot.

JULIAN. I'll just get changed, shall I?

AUDREY. It might be a bit stewed.

JULIAN. I'll just get washed and changed.

AUDREY. You've time for some tea.

> *He exits and leaves coat, hat and brief-case off stage, and re-enters.*

JULIAN. I really am sorry. I nearly burst a blood vessel running for the train.

AUDREY *(has poured)*. Here you are.

JULIAN. You're all dressed up. *(Pause.)* Well you would be, of course. *(Pause.)* I'd have phoned, dear, I really would have phoned, but the meeting went on and on, you see. Then when I did manage to get away, I thought the best thing I could do was just make a bolt for it. Even as it was, as I say, I nearly burst a –

AUDREY. Julian, nobody has suggested that you're late on purpose. Please drink your tea.

JULIAN. Trouble was, there was nobody else to speak for the Geological Section. Hilary Jamieson's off with flu. *(Pause.)* It won't take me a moment to change. I'll just finish my tea and ring the restaurant to alter the booking. Good lord, Audrey, seven-thirty, nine-thirty, what's the difference? *(Pause.)* Or we could go somewhere else. It doesn't have to be the White Tower. I could ring . . . what's that place the snobs go? . . . The Mirabelle. *(Pause.)* If you're sure you still want to go.

AUDREY. Why not?

JULIAN. No reason. None, I just thought, if you were upset, you might prefer . . .

AUDREY. But I'm dressed.

JULIAN. Of course, of course. I'll ring them right away, dear. They can easily change the time.

AUDREY. Don't *you* want to go? We could open a tin, I suppose.

JULIAN. I just thought . . . Sitting about waiting; it might have taken the edge off things. *(Pause.)* I mean one doesn't want to make do. Everything spoiled and rushed. If something's not special on an occasion like this, it's not worth doing. *(Pause.)* Silly of me. *(Pause.)* You're not using our teapot.

AUDREY. In the kitchen?

JULIAN. Oh, I don't know. Things are bought to be used, you know.

AUDREY. We shall use it.

JULIAN. Tea in the kitchen with a Georgian silver tea pot, properly hall marked and attributed to Bellamy. It's rather . . . I mean, one doesn't do appropriate things. It's much more idiosyncratic to use a silver teapot in the kitchen. I rather like the idea. *(Pause.)* I'll ring the restaurant, then.

AUDREY. Stop humouring me, Julian.

JULIAN. What gives you –

AUDREY. Ever since you came in, you've been making small talk. Trying to get me to tell you I don't mind sitting here all dressed up and not knowing what's happened to you. So all right. I do tell you, Julian. I know you couldn't help it. I'm not blaming you. So please get changed and ring the restaurant.

JULIAN. Well, you must mind a little. *(She looks at him sharply.)*

I'd have phoned, dear, if I could. I'd have missed the train though. It was a D.C.P.'s meeting, you see. Somebody from the section had to be there. There was the D.C.P. and the D.D.C.P. and the D.A.D.C.P. – all the top brass, you know. Every section had to be represented. And there was Hilary Jamieson sweating it out in Twickenham with summer 'flu. I did what I could. I made an extremely brief report, and I hope I managed to discourage discussion. Then the moment – the *moment* – the geological section stuff was over, I made my excuses and left. Took a taxi to the station and ran all –

AUDREY. You're not supposed to run. The doctor told you.

JULIAN. I couldn't have known about the meeting.

AUDREY. Nobody's suggesting you could.

JULIAN. Well, I knew there'd be one, of course. I knew there *was* a D.C.P.'s meeting set for today. I didn't tell you because I didn't want to annoy you.

AUDREY. Thank you.

JULIAN. I didn't want to worry you. I couldn't have known –

AUDREY. That Hilary Thing would be ill.

JULIAN. Jamieson.

AUDREY. He was off yesterday. You told me.

JULIAN. He might have come back.

AUDREY. Never mind, Julian. You get changed and *I'll* ring the restaurant.

JULIAN. The trouble was not getting the agenda until this morning. *(He produces it from his jacket pocket.)* I've still got it, actually. Brought it home as a sort of alibi in case you didn't believe me. Really one does behave in the most stereotyped ways. I thought you'd be annoyed. I suppose I was frightened of that. *(Shows her.)* See? Geological Section comes right at the end.

AUDREY. Couldn't they have moved it?

JULIAN. Moved what?

AUDREY. Changed the order? Brought it forward, your thing.

JULIAN. Well – hardly.

AUDREY. Why not?

JULIAN. I don't think one does that, dear.

AUDREY. You mean they never change the order of the agenda?
I don't see why it should matter.

JULIAN. Oh, they do sometimes change the order. I mean, I have
known it happen. If something crops up, or if it's not clear
one will be able to reach important business, or if somebody –

AUDREY. – has to leave early.

JULIAN. I suppose it could be changed.

AUDREY. You said it has been.

JULIAN. I said there are occasions. It's not at all usual.

AUDREY. But it's been done.

JULIAN. Occasionally, I've known it done. One doesn't think
of such a thing oneself.

AUDREY. You mean, *you* don't?

JULIAN. One doesn't disrupt the D.C.P.'s agenda simply for –

AUDREY. One's Silver Wedding day. *(Pause.)* You're too junior,
is that it? They wouldn't take it from you.

JULIAN. Hardly too junior, dear. I think you know my position
well enough.

AUDREY. You have two ways of calling me 'dear'. One is when
you are trying to hurt me, the other is when you're crawling.
It was the second when you came in, and now it's the first.

JULIAN. I'm not trying to hurt you. I'm not trying to attack you
in any way.

AUDREY. Thank you.

JULIAN. But please don't attack me through my job. I am not
junior. I'm not yet head of my Section but I shall be when –

AUDREY. When Hilary Thing dies of summer 'flu.

JULIAN. Jamieson.

AUDREY. Jamieson.

JULIAN. We do important work.

AUDREY. And live in Purley.

JULIAN. What?

AUDREY. The work you do is so important that we live in a semi-detached house in Purley, and when we want to buy a silver teapot for our Silver Wedding, I have to pay for half of it with my own money.

JULIAN. But this is ridiculous. I won't have this argument.

AUDREY. I'm not arguing. I just don't know why you couldn't change the agenda, that's all. *I* went to work at the Advice Bureau this afternoon, and at four-thirty I told Miss Peace –

JULIAN. It's not the same. You make your own hours at the Welfare.

AUDREY. It's work though, isn't it? It's worth doing. Do you think helping people isn't work?

JULIAN *(losing control)*. That's not the point. *(Regaining it.)* I'm sorry, but that's not the point dear. If you'll just stop cross-examining me and accept my word . . .

AUDREY. Cross-examining! You come in. I don't reproach you. I'm prepared to give you the benefit of the doubt.

JULIAN. You've been doing nothing but cross-examine me since I came through that door.

AUDREY. You told me yourself. You brought the agenda home to show me.

JULIAN. Look. We've planned a celebration, dear. Let's not spoil it. Let's just have it.

AUDREY. Are you telling me?

JULIAN. What?

AUDREY. 'We've planned a celebration' – are you telling me that? Look at me, sitting here, dressed up . . .

JULIAN. You didn't have to get dressed so early, dear.

AUDREY. It takes me longer to dress; you know that.

JULIAN. Audrey, dear –

AUDREY. Don't 'dear', me.

JULIAN. Dammit, it's our Silver Wedding Day.

Pause.

AUDREY. Well go on, go on. Ring the White Tower. Get changed. We'll go out. Why not?

JULIAN: For God's sake! . . .

AUDREY. Well, what do you want me to say?

JULIAN. I want you to –

AUDREY. You want me to go out to dinner, just as if nothing had happened. Well, all right. We'll go out to dinner. You've got your way.

JULIAN. There's not much point in going out, if you're going to sulk all through the meal. Spending more than we can afford on food that's going to turn to acid in my stomach.

AUDREY. There's a simple remedy for that, isn't there? Don't upset me and I shan't sulk. When we've arranged a celebration dinner . . .

JULIAN. Audrey . . .

AUDREY. And you've already promised you'll leave work early –

JULIAN. I tried, I tried.

AUDREY. Then don't get into some meeting or other.

JULIAN. I had to be there. I told you there was nobody else to speak for the Geological Section. It was a very important meeting, and the D.C.P. –

AUDREY. Don't D.C.P. me. I'm sick of it. I'm sick and tired of your D.C.P.'s and your important work. You haven't a spark of real ambition, and you cover up by pretending.

JULIAN. There's more to life than ambition.

AUDREY. Such as?

JULIAN. Contentment. I'm doing a serious job in a serious way. It's a worthwhile job; it's cultural. It uses my special capabilities, my special interests. I will not join the rat race for material –

AUDREY. Oh that rat race!

JULIAN. I have believed, I do believe that to be content in one's own –

AUDREY. Content!

JULIAN. In my job, in my job.

AUDREY. Don't shout. Don't raise your voice to me.

JULIAN. I've never pretended to be content at home.

AUDREY. The walls are like paper.

JULIAN. In my job I have a position, I'm valued; I'm respected.

AUDREY. But not enough to change the order of the agenda so that you could get home in time to go out to dinner with your wife on your Silver Wedding day.

JULIAN. Don't push me, dear.

AUDREY. It's 'dear' again, is it?

JULIAN. I said, Don't push me.

AUDREY. Why not?

JULIAN. There are moments in an argument . . . in any argument . . .

AUDREY. Yes?

JULIAN. There are moments at which one should stop.

AUDREY. Why?

JULIAN. Even in marriage – we know this, dear; we know it of old – even in marriage there are . . . necessary reticences, boundaries one doesn't cross if the marriage is to be preserved.

AUDREY. But ours has been preserved, Julian. Twenty-five years. We are preserved. We could hardly be expected to break up now, not after twenty-five years. Where should we go? How should we live? I don't think we need these necessary reticences any longer.

JULIAN. One always needs them. Things that are hurtful . . .

AUDREY. Yes?

JULIAN. Should be suppressed.

AUDREY. But the hurt's out. It's out now. You thought about changing the agenda and you didn't do it. Isn't that right?

JULIAN. It may be.

AUDREY. You could have lifted the phone, and talked to someone's secretary, and done it.

JULIAN. Probably.

AUDREY. Because you're not junior, Julian. You're not nobody. You're a valued and respected member of the staff.

JULIAN. If you put it like that.

AUDREY. But you didn't lift the phone.

JULIAN. No.

AUDREY. You wanted to be late. You wanted to spoil the evening.

JULIAN. Not consciously.

AUDREY. Unconsciously!

JULIAN. Perhaps.

AUDREY. Well now it's conscious. So it's all right for you to be late, it's all right for you to ruin the celebration, but when it comes to asking why, then there are the necessary reticences to be preserved.

JULIAN. Unconsciously I may have been . . . reluctant.

AUDREY. I want to know why.

JULIAN. What is there to celebrate?

    Pause.

AUDREY. You know what.

JULIAN. What do we have to celebrate?

AUDREY. Twenty-five years. We've been together twenty-five years. That's an achievement if nothing else.

    Derisory noise from JULIAN.

Has it been easy for you, then? It's not been easy for me.

JULIAN. Yes. It has. It's been easy. It's not always been pleasant. But, it's been easy. Look at it. Twenty-five years of doing the easier thing. When we got engaged, everybody we knew – everybody who mattered in a place like Teignmouth – they were all expecting it at that time, so it was easier for me to propose than not to, and easier for you to accept than have them wondering if I hadn't proposed.

AUDREY. I shouldn't have accepted if I hadn't –

JULIAN. Loved me?

AUDREY. Liked you. Been fond of you.

JULIAN. Then children.

    She turns away.

If we really wanted one, we could have adopted one. Face it. You don't want a child. And nor do I. It's easier.

AUDREY. I've always been fond of children.

JULIAN. Just as you were fond of me. But it's easier to work in Child Welfare than to have a child and rear it. So you had your work, and I had mine, and the easiest thing was to go on from day to day and come home in the evenings and read and watch television or listen to music in each other's company, because we'd left the West Country behind, and it was too much trouble to make new friends.

AUDREY. You don't suggest we should make friends here? We have friends in London.

JULIAN. But we never see them. It's easier not to. Don't tell me it's not been easy to stay together, Audrey. It's been the easiest thing, it's been the obvious thing. Not always pleasant, that's different.

AUDREY. Don't split hairs.

JULIAN. I'm making a distinction.

AUDREY. Splitting hairs. You've always done it.

JULIAN. I'm making a distinction between what's easy and what's pleasant.

AUDREY. I thought you were telling why you'd spoilt our celebration.

JULIAN. I did tell you. Because there's nothing to celebrate.

AUDREY. We got married. We're still married. That's something.

JULIAN. Not enough.

AUDREY. You're not trying to tell me you've never been happy?

JULIAN. Think about it. When were we happy?

AUDREY. We were happy – at the beginning.

JULIAN. Yes. It was easy then. Sex made it easy.

AUDREY. That's cheap.

JULIAN. No, it's true.

AUDREY. We weren't innocent. You talk as if we were a couple of innocents.

JULIAN. No. We had a wide theoretical knowledge. We were progressive people, and we weren't going to be made miserable by ignorance and we'd read the books. We weren't innocent, but my God we weren't experienced, and when we found out about sex, how wonderful it could be, how we could have as much as we wanted, because we were married –

AUDREY. Julian!

JULIAN. It was so wonderful that we never realized we hadn't a thought or a feeling in common. All the books kept saying we should 'discover' each other; that was the word they all used. It made you feel like Captain Cook. But we didn't discover each other. We just discovered how bloody wonderful sex could be, when secretly we'd both been frightened of it, and we only discovered each *other* when sex wore off, and then we discovered that we didn't really like each other. But it was easier to go on. For twenty-five years.

AUDREY. I've never said I didn't like you.

JULIAN. No, but I've got the message.

AUDREY. You imagine things. *(Looks at her watch.)* There's not much point in phoning now. It's too late.

JULIAN *(begins to gather tea things on tray)*. Yes.

AUDREY. I can make a pilaff. There's some pork left over.

JULIAN. Good.

AUDREY. What are you doing with the tray?

JULIAN. I thought I'd wash up.

AUDREY. Why?

JULIAN. Because I hate you, dear.

    Pause.

AUDREY. I'll dry.

    The sound of the hall clock is heard striking as the lights fade to blackout.

THE DIRECTOR

Come in camera one . . . move in on Matron's glasses. Catch the
glint . . . good.
. . . Camera Two . . . I want a tight up shot of the old woman.
Not that tight. She's dribbling . . . Yeah, that's fine . . . Cut to
two.
Three? Camera three? Line up the son and daughter-in-law
favouring her . . . She's going to yawn. Cut to three. Zoom in on
that yawn. Super!
Cut to two. She's crying! *(To people in the control box.)* Max
is doing a fantastic bloody job . . . Great television! Mustn't make
a meal of it though. *(To studio.)* Mix in one. Have a look at
Matron's hands one . . .
Good.
Camera two. Let me see the old girl's hands . . . Should make a
grainy contrast. I like the way she's pulling out that loose button
. . . super . . . mix in Camera two . . . Great . . .
. . . Sound. Can you bring up that old girl's mike. I want to hear
that wheezing over what matron's saying? . . . Can do? . . .
That's good. No more though or it'll sound like a bloody express
train.
Camera three . . . Wake up camera three! When the son lights
his wife's fag, I want you tight-up. Favour the eyes. I want to
see them screw up . . . Cut to three . . . Late three! It didn't mean
a thing . . . Cut back to two. Pull out to show Max and the old
girl. Good. Hold it there . . .
. . . I'm going to run the film clip in about thirty seconds, Des.
Wind-up, Max. Two, pick-up, Max. Cut in two. Is the clip ready?
Great . . . Run it!

*He relaxes slightly. Takes a drag at a cigarette. He looks at the
monitor. Talks to people in control-box.*

Great idea speeding-up the film, wasn't it? It makes the bed-pan routine look bloody inhuman . . . he's never had such a quick one . . . Hey . . . *(Laughing.)* A bit bloody sick though . . . Des . . . Des? . . . Yeah. Just checking the studio monitors are dead. It'd kill the ward-routine grilling if Matron had seen the film clip . . . Great . . . Another thirty seconds more to run. Alert Max . . . Camera two. I want to come back in on the old girl . . . Yeah . . . Hey has she fallen asleep? Des . . . Des . . . is the old girl asleep? . . . What . . . Dead! Are you sure? But that's great. No, of course we can't show her!

He talks faster and faster.

Camera two on Max. Des tells Max to turn to Matron and the son – the full accusation but and then wind-up bollocking the viewers. Great, great television. Three seconds more film . . . Close in on Max! . . . Cut to two. Wow!!!

RESTING PLACE

by David Campton

The scene is a cemetery. There is the sound of birds, with the noise of traffic in the distance.

An old couple are discovered sitting on a bench. It is late afternoon in autumn.

OLD WOMAN. It's a long way.

OLD MAN. It gets longer.

OLD WOMAN. I'm glad of a sit down. Half way. Good of them to set a bench here. Where we can watch the flowers.

OLD MAN. What have we got for tea?

OLD WOMAN. All the year round.

OLD MAN. I'm ready for my tea.

OLD WOMAN. Spring. Summer. Autumn. Winter. Not many places in this town where you can see flowers in winter, except in the shops. But you can't sit down in the shops. I'm glad we came this way from the shops. Where we can sit in the sun, and watch the flowers. Here, in the cemetery.

OLD MAN. Can't stay long.

OLD WOMAN. We're lucky to have a cemetery on the way home.

OLD MAN. Are we?

OLD WOMAN. It's so peaceful.

OLD MAN. Before long the bell's going to ring, and the man'll blow his whistle to tell us he's closing the gates. *(He looks at the* OLD WOMAN.*)*

> *The* OLD WOMAN *shows no sign of moving.*

Then he's going to lock the gates. *(Pause.)* We ought to be home before then. *(Pause.)* Having tea.

OLD WOMAN. There's no place quite as peaceful as a cemetery.

OLD MAN. Can't climb over the railings the way I used to.

OLD WOMAN. It's the angels.

OLD MAN. You and your angels.

OLD WOMAN. An angel's very nice.

OLD MAN *(peering over into the shopping bag)*. What's in the bag?

OLD WOMAN. All in white. With a hand raised.

OLD MAN. There's things in that bag I don't know about.

OLD WOMAN. Holding a palm leaf. There's something comforting about an angel holding a palm leaf.

OLD MAN. I saw you pick up something on the side. I saw you out of the corner of my eye while I was at the 'bacca counter. You slipped it into the bag.

OLD WOMAN. A plain headstone has its points. Or an urn with garlands. But there's something special about a white marble angel. An angel's a reminder. *(Slaps his hand away from shopping bag.)* Don't fidget.

OLD MAN. Is it sausages?

OLD WOMAN. No, it's not.

OLD MAN. Or a bit of ham?

OLD WOMAN. Eyes like needles, you've got.

OLD MAN. Pork pie?

OLD WOMAN. If you must know, it's a pair of kippers.

OLD MAN. Kippers, eh?

OLD WOMAN. It's been a long time since we had a nice kipper.

OLD MAN. I like kippers.

OLD WOMAN. That's why I got 'em. I said to myself, we'll have a proper Saturday tea today. We'll have pikelets and strawberry jam.

OLD MAN. And kippers.

OLD WOMAN. Yes. There's something special about an angel. White marble catches the sun.

OLD MAN. It'll soon be setting.

OLD WOMAN. Peaceful. You couldn't find a pleasanter cemetery if you looked. Everywhere so tidy, look at that heap of flowers over there. Orchids.

OLD MAN. Orchids at a funeral? They'll be having champagne next.

OLD WOMAN. Orchids!

OLD MAN. Ah! You know now who it is, don't you?

OLD WOMAN. We don't know anybody who could afford orchids.

OLD MAN. It's Fred Turtle. The bookie.

OLD WOMAN. Fred Turtle? Is he dead?

OLD MAN. They've just buried him.

OLD WOMAN. Fred Turtle! But there was no age in the man. Couldn't have been a day over seventy.

OLD MAN. Had his moneysworth while he lived, though. Wine, women, *and* song. A right voice he had.

OLD WOMAN. Splashing money like water. Orchids. He's with his wife again now.

OLD MAN. First time for fifty years they've been together without fighting.

OLD WOMAN. I wonder when they'll put the headstone back. It'll have his name on then as well as hers. 'Fred and Miranda Turtle. In their death they were not divided.'

OLD MAN. Now, love . . .

OLD WOMAN. 'In their . . .'

OLD MAN. Don't start on that again.

OLD WOMAN. Which is more than will be said of some folk I know.

OLD MAN. We shouldn't have stopped here. It sets you off every time.

OLD WOMAN. Where are they going to put *us*, eh?

OLD MAN. It's too late in the day to think about that. Past teatime.

OLD WOMAN. Where are they going to put us? In some hole that nobody else wants.

OLD MAN. Try thinking about something else. Think about the kippers.

OLD WOMAN. Down by the railway lines, I shouldn't wonder. Down where nobody ever goes. And they'll stick you in another old hole. On your own. Parted after all these years.

OLD MAN. When we're both gone, what will it matter?

F

OLD WOMAN. Buried with strangers. It's indecent. I wouldn't even mind not having an angel. Not much. A simple slab to let them know who's underneath.

OLD MAN. We can't afford it. We can't even afford the grave. Not a whole grave. To ourselves.

OLD WOMAN. Though I'd prefer an angel, of course.

OLD MAN. They cost so much.

OLD WOMAN. An angel, holding a book.

OLD MAN. Hundreds of pounds. We haven't got hundreds of pounds.

OLD WOMAN. And on the book written, 'Jim and Minnie. In their death they were not divided'. But they will be. *(Pause.)* If we'd got the money, we could be together. For ever and ever.

OLD MAN. We haven't got the money. We never had it.
(Pause.)

OLD WOMAN. Whose fault was that?

OLD MAN. It's an old story, Min. Let it rest.

OLD WOMAN. If you'd been a millionaire you could have bought a grave of your own, with angels all round. You could have built a family vault if you'd been a millionaire.

OLD MAN. I wasn't cut out to be a millionaire.

OLD WOMAN. Fred Turtle made money. He hadn't a quarter your brain, but he made it. Without his wife's help either. Economy? She didn't know the meaning of the word. But there they lie together, smothered in orchids, just waiting for the headstone.

OLD MAN. I couldn't make money.

OLD WOMAN. I told you how. Time and again I told you. You didn't want to make money, that was your trouble.

OLD MAN. I was a shoemaker, I made shoes.

OLD WOMAN. You should have made money.

OLD MAN. In all the years we've been married, you never had wet feet.

OLD WOMAN. You could have been a butcher. Butchers make

money. Don't I know it. The price of a bit of liver; and what doesn't pass over the counter ends up as sausages. Unless they eat it themselves; which is always a saving. I could have been a millionaire on what I saved if you'd been a butcher.

OLD MAN. I couldn't see myself as anything but a shoemaker.

OLD WOMAN. If only you'd listened to me, I could have made you a millionaire.

OLD MAN. I didn't know you wanted me to be a millionaire. I thought you were just nagging.

OLD WOMAN. Nagging!

Slight pause.

OLD MAN. You married the wrong man.

OLD WOMAN. I did my best to push you on, and you call it nagging.

OLD MAN. You should have married a man who could make money. Like Fred Turtle. I was never any good at making it; spending it was all I knew about. But I spent it on you. Flowers when there were flowers to be had; yards of dress stuff when they weren't. I was satisfied with a leather apron, but you were always dressed. If you wanted a man to make money instead of spending it, you should have married a different man.

OLD WOMAN. If you didn't want me to push, why did you ask me to marry you?

OLD MAN. That's all you think about. A headstone.

OLD WOMAN. What else is there to think about?

OLD MAN. There's me.

OLD WOMAN. You won't have a headstone either.

OLD MAN. I'm not talking about a headstone.

OLD WOMAN. What are you talking about then?

OLD MAN. Me.

OLD WOMAN. You?

OLD MAN. You're telling me I've wasted all my time.

OLD WOMAN. What else have you done with it?

A bell begins to strike slowly. At the first clang their argument is cut short.

They sit in silence as the bell tolls. It stops.
Pause.

It happened again.

OLD MAN. It happens every time. *(Pause.)* Aren't you ever going to be able to forget?

OLD WOMAN. It gets colder.

OLD MAN. Hold my hand. *(He takes the* OLD WOMAN's *hand.)*

OLD WOMAN. That was the bell.

OLD MAN. Don't let's come this way again.

In the distance a whistle is blown.

OLD WOMAN. That's the man with his whistle.

OLD MAN. Locking up.

OLD WOMAN. Better be moving. *(Pause.)* Come on.

OLD MAN. I suppose it's too late to be a millionaire now.

Pause.

OLD WOMAN. There's kippers for tea.

OLD MAN. Kippers, eh?

OLD WOMAN. And pikelets and strawberry jam.

OLD MAN. I like a nice kipper.

They pick up the shopping bag between them, and start to walk away.

The OLD WOMAN *pauses, and looks back towards the pile of flowers.*

OLD WOMAN. Orchids! . . . You can't beat a kipper. And a strong cup of tea.

The OLD MAN *gently draws her away.*

OLD MAN. No, there's nothing like a kipper. And a cup of strong tea.

They wander away as lights fade to blackout.

Appendix

THE HEADMASTER*

He is very angry. The audience are the boys. Perhaps one of the 'stable doors' could be opened to show a shelf with cups and a photograph of a team.

Ye Gods and little fishes! Beaten thirty-six nil by a pestilential day school who wear vests under their rugger shirts.

He paces back and forth, shooting out his cuffs and easing his collar with his forefinger.

Esprit de corps! Keenness! That's what matters! How can we hope to attract the right sort of father to send his boy here on today's showing! Beaten thrity-six nil by the sons of fish-cake manufacturers who can't even speak the Queen's English!

More pacing.

Guts! Not a word you'd use in the drawing-room, but my godfathers it's what you need on the rugger field. On this afternoon's showing you've as much guts as a bunch of anaemic schoolgirls. You were like pimply youths in velvet suits doing crochet in deck chairs!

More pacing

And on the touch-line. It's a proud tradition here that turning out to cheer on the school is voluntary, but I'll want an explanation from every boy who wasn't there, and don't think a cold is an excuse. You shouldn't catch colds. Anyone with a cold will be beaten twice. Once for not turning out and once for catching a cold.

And for those who did condescend to support the school team the cheering was pathetic . . . pathetic. You should be hoarse . . . Are you hoarse boy? Are you? Anyone who isn't hoarse will be

* This linking sketch and the one that follows were not used in the production of *Mixed Doubles* at the Comedy Theatre. They can, however, be substituted for two of the other linking sketches, e.g. *The Headmaster* for *The Doctor* or *The Advertising Man* for *The Union Official*.

beaten too. Ye Gods it sounded more like a dowager's bun fight than a vital fixture.

More pacing.

Team spirit – that's what makes a house cock-house and a school worth its salt. Team spirit, not individual brilliance. It's not what you learn in the classroom that will count in later life. It's how long you can hug the ball under the boots of the whole enemy pack.

More pacing, but less agitated. When he speaks it's almost mildly.

Learn to play games and you'll grow up to be men. It's through games you'll learn honour, loyalty, manliness, the will to succeed, the ability to give and receive orders, discipline and generosity. In my experience rugger, cricket and possibly Latin prose are all an Englishman really needs to know about.

A pause.

I shall now beat the entire school starting with the captain of the first fifteen . . .

Fade.

THE ADVERTISING MAN

A creative think-in at an advertising agency. The HEAD MAN *is addressing his (invisible) colleagues. He has a modern swivel-chair in tubular chrome and ox-hide but is standing-up to emote. He wears a polo-neck sweater, hipster trousers, and bootees. His hair is arranged like the Emperor Nero. He is a little too hip and frantic for his age (forty-seven). He is holding two or three mock-ups which, having verbally destroyed them, he throws down. He has the hetero-pseudo-queer voice of the trendier end of communications.*

Darling hearts I don't want to put you down but Christ . . .

He looks at the first mock-up. He reads:

'My mum's as hip as they come' – Well mum may be, but whoever dreamt that one up is as square as a pineapple chunk. Swinging London's dead remember. Even the suburbs have turned onto that by now – all that admass floral tie bit's a bad scene. So we all had a ball at the Ad Lib but baby that's all over now. Right?

He throws it down and looks at the next.

'Make the Joneses keep up with you' – The affluent bit! Envy buying! You've got to be joking. Whatever happened to Harold Macmillan?

He throws that one down and paces about smoking.

Think creatively. Think about the product. Who needs it? – no-one but who do we want to think they need it? – the budgie belt; right? What's the image. What's the message. They can afford it – right? But it'll need a bit of sacrifice, or they won't feel it's worth it! – Who are they? Not A, Not B? – Hey, they don't exist in consumer technology. Not yet. We're pioneers. Frontier-men. It should be a challenge, a breakthrough in creative advertising.

More pacing.

What do they read? Small ads for army surplus blankets,

directoire knickers, garden sheds – write to box number 123, money back if dissatisfied . . . Are you hip to that scene?

More pacing.

We want the small ads out there on the big posters. We want the box-number mentality catered for on the sixty-second Telly commercials.

Where's it at? In those houses you only see from trains. That's where it's at. Think square – Wait a minute. That's not bad, not bad at all! *THINK SQUARE.*

Let's put it in a glass of false teeth and see if it gets the stains off.

Methuen's Modern Plays

EDITED BY JOHN CULLEN

Shelagh Delaney	*A Taste of Honey*
	The Lion in Love
Max Frisch	*The Fire Raisers*
	Andorra
Jean Giraudoux	*Tiger at the Gates*
	Duel of Angels
Rolf Hochhuth	*The Representative*
Heinar Kipphardt	*In the Matter of J. Robert Oppenheimer*
Arthur Kopit	*Chamber Music and other plays*
Jakov Lind	*The Silver Foxes are Dead and other plays*
Henry Livings	*Eh?*
John Mortimer	*The Judge*
Joe Orton	*Crimes of Passion*
	Loot
	What the Butler Saw
Harold Pinter	*The Birthday Party*
	The Room and The Dumb Waiter
	The Caretaker
	A Slight Ache and other plays
	The Collection and The Lover
	The Homecoming
	Tea Party and other plays
	Landscape and Silence
Jean-Paul Sartre	*Crime Passionnel*
Theatre Workshop and Charles Chilton	*Oh What A Lovely War*

★   ★   ★

Methuen Playscripts

Paul Ableman	*Tests*
	Blue Comedy
Barry Bermange	*Nathan and Tabileth and Oldenberg*

Methuen's Theatre Classics